POWER AND THE PRESIDENCY

POWER AND THE PRESIDENCY

★

EDITED BY ROBERT A. WILSON

PUBLICAFFAIRS

NEW YORK

LIBRARY OF CONGRESS CATALOGING-IN-PUBLICATION DATA

Power and the presidency / edited by Robert A. Wilson. — 1st ed.

p. cm.

Includes index.

Contents: Preface/by Robert A. Wilson—Power and the presidency/David McCullough—
Franklin D. Roosevelt/Doris Kearns Goodwin—Dwight D. Eisenhower and John F. Kennedy/
Michael R. Beschloss—Lyndon B. Johnson/Robert A. Caro—Richard M. Nixon/Benjamin
C. Bradlee—Ronald Reagan/Edmund Morris—William J. Clinton/David Maraniss.

ISBN 1–891620–43–6

1. Presidents—United States—History—20th century. 2. Executive Power—United States—
History—20th century. 3. United States—Politics and government—1933–1945. 4. United
States—Politics and government—1945–1989. 5. United States—Politics and govern-
ment—1989– I. Wilson, Robert A., 1941–

E176.1.P883 2000

973'099—dc21

99–055287

Book design by Jenny Dossin.

FIRST EDITION

1 3 5 7 9 10 8 6 4 2

TO

SHEILA CUNNINGHAM

with gratitude for the gift of her extraordinary friendship,

RICHARD FLOOR

for his generosity and loyalty,

AND

JOSEPH MARK WILSON

for his example.

★

CONTENTS

★

Seeing is believing. It's the one axiom a contender for our nation's presidency and the immense power it confers on a single citizen can't leave home without. Because it is in the mind's eye and private reveries that the belief must take hold, beginning with a rhetorical question—"Why not me?"—or one just slightly less self-centered: "If not me, who?" Not surprisingly, those most susceptible to seeing and believing themselves in the Oval Office are government insiders, especially those inside the Senate. It has been said that almost all senators at one time or another hear in their inner ears "Hail to the Chief" played for them, although only two of the eleven presidents since FDR served in the Senate.

While we like the idea of the office seeking the person, it doesn't work that way with the exception of military figures associated closely with the leadership of a war: Washington, Grant, Eisenhower. The person has to have much, much more than an itch for the office and its power; it takes a mania and the capacity for the punishment of having life and family turned inside out in the blood sport search for all sins of omission and commission. Not to mention the endless indignity of fund-raising and the requirement to take absurdity (i.e., the Iowa and New Hampshire primaries) with a straight face.

One question that generally causes presidential candidates trouble as their quest begins is the most straightforward: "Why do you want to be president?" What makes it a tough question is that the real answer—some version of "I want the power"—may be just a little too candid. Nevertheless, the magnitude of presidential power and what can be done with it accounts for the depth of desire required to run a brutal gauntlet that can now last not just for months but for years.

The idea of having a distinguished array of historians, biographers, and journalists address the subject of power and the presidency was born in the spring of 1998 in a series of conversations I had with James Wright, Dartmouth College teacher, historian, provost, and now president. With the help of the Montgomery Endowment at Dartmouth, the initiative was launched. In the winter and spring terms of 1999, we brought an extraordinary group of presidential historians and biographers and journalists to campus as Montgomery Fellows for a series of lectures before overflow crowds, which were then broadcast by C-SPAN. The essays in this volume were adapted from those lectures.

All of the participants have intimate knowledge of modern presidential history. Some have studied and writ-

★

Preface

ten about several administrations. Some have particular knowledge of a single president. All brought their profoundly personal perspectives and informed judgment to bear on how these most powerful men in the world wielded, and sometimes dissipated, the enormous power and influence of both the office and the force of their individual personalities.

Certain common themes emerge. There is, clearly, the huge importance of connecting with us—the ability of the president to inspire and inform the nation. Franklin Roosevelt, John Kennedy, and Ronald Reagan were masterful in summoning the full power of language, metaphors, and stories, each in his own way. In fact, the differences among presidential styles are striking. The spectrum ranges from Theodore Roosevelt's open delight in exercising power on a worldwide stage; to Lyndon Johnson's unparalleled genius for twisting congressional arms to get what he wanted; to Richard Nixon's tendency, at least on the domestic front, to focus his power against his enemies, both real and imagined, in sometimes mean and eventually unlawful ways.

In his overview of presidential power, which opened the lecture series and also starts this book, David McCullough observes that although most presidents have professed no liking for the job, "rare was the man who truly wished to let go his hold on the office. Most would have fought to their last breath to stay if they could." The allure of presidential power surely lies at the heart of the reason why. Power—how it is used and to what ends—defines a president's legacy and his place in history.

For the light they shed on power and the presidency, I am most grateful to the seven authors who participated in this initiative. The lecture series also benefited from the insights of the extraordinary filmmaker David Grubin, whose presidential documentaries are without equal. Merrill McLoughlin's editorial insights were especially perceptive.

Each of the Montgomery Fellows involved in *Power and the Presidency*, during their stay, became part of the Dartmouth community: lecturing, meeting formally and informally with students and faculty, listening and learning from each other. Barbara Gerstner, who directs the Montgomery Endowment Programs, deserves full credit for creating an atmosphere that encourages the energy of such interactions.

I am indebted to Jim Wright, whose commitment was crucial to our success, and to Harle Montgomery and the Montgomery Endowment. The Montgomerys' philanthropy reflects the discerning taste and thoughtful patriotism of both Harle and her late husband, Ken, whose spirit infuses all that the endowment makes possible.

ROBERT A. WILSON

Dallas, Texas
October 1999

CHAPTER ONE

POWER AND
THE PRESIDENCY

WHAT'S ESSENTIAL IS INVISIBLE

BY DAVID MCCULLOUGH

★

At the heart of history, and a great part of the pull of history, is the mystery of human nature. Human nature—individual personality, makeup, call it what you will—has to be reckoned as a prime force in any consideration of the presidency and its power.

There is a scene in Antoine de Saint-Exupéry's *The Little Prince* when the fox says that what's essential is invisible. And so it is with this large subject of presidential power: To a very large extent it is invisible. It has to do with aspects of individual personality for which there are no ready measurements—the integrity of George Washington, Abraham Lincoln's depth of soul, the courage of Harry Truman. Or think of the charm of John F. Kennedy at a press conference or Ronald Reagan in front of a television camera in almost any circumstance.

And what a disparate group of personalities has held the office! We have had farmers and generals, a great many lawyers, a college president, a world-famous engineer, numerous career politicians, and a movie star; and the movie star was by no means the only actor—or necessarily the best actor. Six of our presidents—and they were all men, all white men, to be more specific—came from

Ohio. There have been a number of Episcopalians, still more Presbyterians, and one Roman Catholic.

Abraham Lincoln was the tallest, at six foot four. James Madison was the smallest, at five foot four and weighed only a hundred pounds. In striking contrast, William Howard Taft, by far the largest of the lot, weighed 336 pounds. A custom-built bathtub had to be installed for him in the White House. In a wonderful old photograph, the three workmen who did the installation sit together quite comfortably in Taft's giant tub. With Taft we had gravitas of a kind, if not necessarily power, such as seen never before or since.

Calvin Coolidge is famous for having said as little as possible. Theodore Roosevelt could hardly keep quiet. Theodore Roosevelt was the youngest president in history. When he took office, after the death of McKinley in 1901, he was all of forty-two.

TR was the first president born in a big city. Harry Truman was the first and only president born in Missouri and the only president in this century who never went to college. It was not until Jimmy Carter that we had a president who was born in a hospital. John Adams, first of the Harvard men, lived to be the oldest president ever. He was ninety at the time of his death in 1826.

Of the first seven presidents, whose combined terms spanned forty-eight years, all were slave masters but two, and they were father and son, John and John Quincy Adams. So for nearly half a century, slaveholders dominated in the executive branch.

With few exceptions, they've all done a good deal of complaining about the job and professed no liking for it. It has been so from the beginning. George Washington went to his place at the head of the new government, "accompanied," he said, "by feelings not unlike those of a culprit who is going to the place of his execution." John Adams, Washington's successor, describing his inauguration to his wife, Abigail, wrote, "A solemn scene it was indeed and it was made more affecting to me by the presence of the General [Washington], whose countenance was as serene and unclouded as the day. Methought I heard him say, 'Aye, I am fairly out and you are fairly in. See which of us is the happiest.'"

Jefferson famously declared the presidency a "splendid misery." Andrew Jackson called it "dignified slavery." Polk said it was "no bed of roses." Abraham Lincoln thought himself unfit for the role. Grover Cleveland told a very young Franklin Delano Roosevelt when they met, "Boy, I hope you will never, ever become president." Harry Truman said no one in his right mind would want the job if he knew what it entailed and privately referred to the White House as "the great white jail."

Going back to George Washington's homesickness for

Mount Vernon, nearly all have longed to return to whence they came, or so they said. But then rare was the man who truly wished to let go his hold on the office. Most would have fought to their last breath to stay if they could.

Only Teddy Roosevelt openly declared his love for the job. "Nobody ever enjoyed the presidency as I did," he boasted, and by all evidence that was so.

As John Steinbeck once wrote, "We give the President more work than a man can do, more responsibility than a man should take, more pressure than a man can bear." But we also give him more power, far more power, than has been held by any mortals in all history and a commensurate lot of swash, the perks and show of power, to go with it. No king of England, no oriental potentate of old ever arrived with greater display of his importance than does the modern president of the United States—which is a long way from Thomas Jefferson's walking to the Capitol for his inauguration.

Here are some present-day statistics about the office: It pays $200,000 a year—taxable—but includes an annual expense allowance of $50,000, which is nontaxable. Then there's an additional expense account of $12,000 for official entertaining and a $100,000 travel allowance.

The executive branch, which includes all cabinet-level positions and those departments, numbers 2.75 million people whose payroll comes to $9.25 billion. The White

House staff, that is the immediate staff of the president—what in Jefferson's day was a half dozen or so—is now 382 at a cost of $1.64 million.

The perks include a helicopter, Air Force One and Air Force Two, and a fleet of thirty-five limousines. There is a White House swimming pool, tennis court, gymnasium, bowling alley, and as of the Clinton years a jogging track. The president also has two movie theaters, recording facilities, and a library. There are riding horses supplied by the army, should he wish them; a private, armor-plated Pullman car; and some several hundred Secret Service agents on call for his protection.

He and his family live rent-free, it should be noted. Annual maintenance and operation of the White House runs to $8 million and requires still another staff of more than a hundred maids, cooks, butlers, gardeners, and electricians. There is a director of systems manager for electronic mail, a director of the gift unit, a deputy director of White House gifts, and a manager of data entry night force, among others.

Then there's Camp David, which several presidents have hardly used at all. Harry Truman, for instance, thought it boring and wanted never to go there. The cost of Camp David is approximately $1 million a year.

One of the best indices of what's happened to the scale of operations in recent years is the presidential trip to

China, which seems to have become obligatory. According to the *New York Times,* when Richard Nixon first went to China in 1972, his retinue numbered 300. Three years later, when Gerald Ford made the trip, 450 went along. By 1984, when Ronald Reagan went, he took 600. Then came a temporary dip in the curve in 1989, when those accompanying George Bush numbered 500. But in 1998, when Clinton made the trip, more than 1,000 went with him.

The twentieth-century presidency begins with Theodore Roosevelt. He was like nobody who had ever been president before and appeared on the scene just as the century was getting under way. Significantly, it was also at the point when it became technically possible to reproduce photographs in newspapers and magazines. So Roosevelt immediately became the most photographed president in history until then—and usually in action, this made possible by improved camera technique. He was photographed with his family, jumping his horse, hiking, playing tennis. James J. Hill, the railroad tycoon, who didn't care for Roosevelt, said all he ever did was pose for pictures and draw his pay.

Modern times caught up with the presidency during TR's tenure. He was the first president to go down in a submarine, the first to go up in an airplane, the first to call it the White House officially. Most important, he saw himself as a *world* leader. America had no choice but to play a lead part in the world, he preached.

He embraced the power of the presidency without hesitation and with open delight, and he used it effectively and imaginatively. He said he liked power for what he could do with it. "While president, I have been president emphatically," he said.

Eager to display American sea power, he decided to send the fleet on a goodwill tour around the world. Told that Congress would refuse to appropriate the money, he said he had sufficient funds at hand to send the ships halfway; then it would be up to Congress to decide whether to bring them home again.

To many, TR is the president who built the Panama Canal. He himself thought it was what he would be best remembered for—and understandably. The canal was the biggest-ever American effort beyond our borders and a project of worldwide importance. In fact, it was one of the greatest of American achievements, for which that whole generation rightfully took tremendous pride. No other country had either the will or the wherewithal to do such a mighty thing, it was said, or a man like the one in the White House to see that it was done right.

When Roosevelt went to Panama to inspect the work firsthand in 1906, it marked the first time a president had ever left the country while in office. And as might be expected, he went by battleship. The days he toured the "diggings" were among the happiest of his life and can be seen now as a kind of set piece—a president perfectly cast for his time. The spectacle, like nothing seen anywhere on earth before, was of American know-how, American machinery, American money and political power accomplishing what nature had neglected to provide: "the dream of Columbus," a passage to India.

Roosevelt was photographed his every waking hour on the scene. It was the first great presidential photo opportunity in history, and one picture has become a metaphor for the age. As possibly only he could, TR took the controls of a giant 95-ton Bucyrus-Erie steam shovel while wearing a white linen suit. And so there he is as commander in chief at the helm of "the biggest work that's ever been done," as he told the Americans on the job.

But it should be remembered, too, that he'd "taken" the isthmus with a high-handed use of power against the nation of Colombia. As he said in a speech, "I took the isthmus, started the canal and then left Congress not to debate the canal, but to debate me." There's a raw kind of arrogance to that. There's also a raw truth to it. And the country, as it happened, loved it. He was the most popular president we had had until then, and few since have had quite the same kind of hold on the popular imagination.

He gave the country a good time just being himself. But importantly, he *used* his popularity. He didn't just want it for the sake of being popular; it was power he could make use of.

At the time of the great anthracite coal strike of 1902, TR stepped in as no president had, brought the executive branch of the government into labor arbitration for the first time, settled the strike, and transformed labor relations thereafter. But then he entered into almost everything. In nearly eight years in office, he initiated the first successful antitrust suit against a corporate monopoly. He doubled the size of the navy; helped settle the Russo-Japanese War; established five national parks, including the Grand Canyon; and made conservation a popular cause for the first time.

It's often remarked that the great presidents have been those who served in times of crisis. And that might be taken as the rule, were it not for the stunning exception of Theodore Roosevelt, who was president when there was no crisis, when, in fact, he could easily have coasted. But he was Theodore Roosevelt, and that's the point. He was ebullient, confident, full of ideas, interested in everything, seldom without a book. He read books; he wrote books. He wrote his own letters. He wrote his own messages to Congress. He wrote his own speeches.

Maybe if we could put presidential power in a pot and

boil it all down, a big part of what we would find at the bottom would be language, the use of language, the potency of words. Power to persuade is power indeed, and only a relative few of the presidents have had it—Lincoln, Teddy Roosevelt, Woodrow Wilson, and Franklin Roosevelt. And JFK. His inaugural address didn't just thrill the country at the time; it still does. The language transcends time.

Sometimes just a line—a single line—spoken by a president can do wonders. Remember, for example, when at his inaugural Jimmy Carter said, "For myself and for our nation, I want to thank my predecessor for all he has done to heal our land." What a moment it was for the country. It got the new Carter administration off to exactly the right start. The glow of good feeling wouldn't last long, but there it was, and it was just what was needed.

One of my favorite lines from an inaugural address is this: "How can we love our country and not love our countrymen? And loving them, reach out a hand when they fall, heal them when they're sick, and provide opportunities to make them self-sufficient so they will be equal in fact and not just in theory." It was said by Ronald Reagan.

Kennedy almost never talked about himself. The first-personal singular almost never entered into anything he said, in contrast to so many others since. It was a big part of his appeal. Theodore Roosevelt not only called the presidency the "bully pulpit," but he demonstrated that the pulpit is the essence of the power of the office. Harry Truman was saying much the same thing when, in a fit of exasperation, he tried to dismiss the whole notion of presidential power:

> Aside from the impossible administrative burden, he, the President, has to take all sorts of abuse from liars and demagogues. The people can never understand why the President does not use his supposedly great power to make them behave. Well, all the President is is a glorified public relations man who spends his time flattering, kissing and kicking people to get them to do what they are supposed to do anyway.

Truman was neither brilliant nor eloquent. He did not have the gift to move the country with words; to lift us up to do something bigger, nobler; to rise to a "rendezvous with destiny," the way his predecessor, Franklin Roosevelt, could. FDR was extraordinary in that way through the worst depression in history and the most terrible of wars. And it was then, almost overnight as history goes, that the size, the scope, the expenditures of government grew by geometric proportions, and with them the importance—or power—of the presidency.

What is so difficult for many today to understand is that in the 1930s the United States was neither rich nor a military power. The army stood twenty-sixth in the world in strength, behind Switzerland and Argentina. A good 40 percent of all the families in America were living on incomes of less than $1,000 a year. The whole idea of a rich, all-powerful nation-state with a standing army surpassing that of any on earth is something relatively new to American life.

With Truman's presidency in 1945 came the advent of nuclear weapons and, soon after, the cold war, the creation of the CIA, the National Security Council, a burgeoning Defense Department, NATO, and a fearsome, stepped-up arms race with the Soviets. As Truman saw the presidency, his chief responsibility was to make the decisions, and he made some of the most difficult and far-reaching of any president. If not brilliant or eloquent, he was courageous and principled. The invisible something he brought to the office was character.

He also demonstrated, and dramatically at times, what power—he would have said "authority"—rests with the president constitutionally, how much a president can accomplish by signing his name. His most sensational and controversial decision was to fire General Douglas MacArthur, which he did on the perfectly sound premise, as set forth in the Constitution, that no one but the president is commander in chief of the armed forces. His subordinate, MacArthur, was flagrantly disobeying orders—

indeed, if you go over the record, you wonder that Truman didn't fire him sooner. Outrage in the country was stupendous. MacArthur was an authentic American hero, the greatest American of his day, many passionately believed. Who was little Harry Truman to bring him down? The answer, of course, was that Harry Truman was president, and in time the country would come to see that he had done the right thing, even in the face of seeing his popularity plummet.

Another notable example of courageous executive authority—again at great risk of popularity—was the executive order that made segregation in the armed forces illegal. The year was 1948, an election year. Friends and advisers warned Truman privately that if he persisted in his civil rights program, he was certain to lose in November. If that were so, Truman responded, then he would be losing for a good cause. He had no need to go to Congress. He had only to take up his pen—and he did.

Another brave and controversial exercise of presidential power was Gerald Ford's decision to pardon Richard Nixon, which to my mind, was also the right thing to do— not for Ford's political fortunes but for the country.

The power of the presidency and the long-range wisdom of several of our presidents may be found also in the power they did not exercise. We don't give enough credit to presidents for what they don't do. John Adams did not go to war with France at a time when a great part of the country was breathing fire for war. Politically, it would have been the easy path and greatly to Adams's advantage. But he knew a war was the last thing the struggling new country needed and refused to go along. Truman didn't use the atomic bomb in Korea in the face of tremendous pressure to do so. Eisenhower didn't go into Vietnam. These were vastly important decisions.

Sometimes I wonder if we make too much of our presidents. Might it be better if we ignored them a little more than we do? Yet I don't think we can ever know enough about them, particularly before putting them in the job. The truth is, of course, it makes an enormous difference who's in the White House.

John Adams was the first president to occupy the White House, the first to live there, though it was not for long. He moved from the executive mansion at Philadelphia to the new quarters in Washington in November of 1801, shortly after he was defeated for a second term by Thomas Jefferson. An idea of the size of the executive branch then can be drawn from the fact that the presidential files he brought with him were packed in seven cartons—less than some of us pack for a summer vacation.

The White House was still unfinished. Only about half the rooms had been plastered, and much of what had been plastered was still wet. Fires were going in the fireplaces to dry these rooms. The whole place smelled of wet plaster and fresh paint. Floors were strewn with carpenters' tools. Outside stood piles of construction rubble.

Adams arrived unannounced by coach, accompanied by his secretary, William Shaw, and a single servant. That night, after supper, he took a candle, mounted the one staircase in use, and went to bed. The following day, he wrote a letter to Abigail, two lines from which Franklin Roosevelt had carved into the mantel in the state dining room.

> I pray Heaven bestow the best blessing on this house and all that shall hereafter inhabit it. May none but honest and wise men ever rule under this roof.

It was a good prayer then; it is a good prayer still.

CHAPTER TWO

FRANKLIN D. ROOSEVELT

"SUBLIME CONFIDENCE"

BY DORIS KEARNS GOODWIN

★

My interest in the presidency was rooted in the privilege of knowing closely one president, Lyndon Baines Johnson, when I was a twenty-four-year-old White House intern. In the months leading up to my selection as a White House fellow, I had been a graduate student at Harvard, actively involved in the antiwar movement, and I had written an article that came out in the *New Republic* just before we were to start work. Its title: "How to Remove Lyndon Johnson." I was certain that he would kick me out of the program. But surprisingly, he said, "Oh, bring her down here for a year, and if I can't win her over, no one can." So I ended up working for him in the White House the last year of his presidency and then accompanied him to his ranch in the last four years of his life to help with his memoirs.

I never fully understood why he had chosen me for those months of talking. I like to believe it was because I was a good listener and he was a great storyteller—perhaps the best I've ever known. He could mimic people's voices. He could keep your attention for hours. Half of his stories weren't true, but they were great nonetheless.

I realize now what an extraordinary privilege it was to spend so much time with this aging lion of a man, who was trying to understand what had happened in his life, the war in Vietnam having cut his presidency in two. For in the vulnerable state he found himself in during those last years, he opened up to me in ways I suspect he never would have had I known him at the height of his power. I'd like to believe that privilege fired within me the drive to understand the inner person behind the public figure that I've tried to bring to each of my books, most particularly to my study of Franklin Roosevelt.

In the historians' polls, Franklin Roosevelt consistently ranks among the top three presidents, along with George Washington and Abraham Lincoln, for having led the American people successfully through two major crises of the twentieth century, depression and war, while not only preserving but strengthening democracy at a time when the other nations of the world often turned to fascism or communism. So let me begin at the beginning, with a portrait of America in 1933, when Roosevelt became president.

"The great knife of the Depression," one historian wrote, "had cut through the entire population, cleaving open the lives of rich and poor alike." The experience was so nearly universal that it approached in its elemental shock the primary experiences of birth and death: one out of four Americans without jobs, vast numbers without enough income to eat, vast numbers unable to keep their homes, unable to pay the mortgage or to provide the basic necessities for their families.

By the time Roosevelt became president, we were in the third year of this Great Depression, and there was little sign of its letting up. Herbert Hoover, a decent man, had tried his best to cope, but he was hamstrung by a conservative economic orthodoxy: the belief that the federal government could not intervene in private markets; that public debt would undermine the economic health of the nation just as private debt undermined the economic health of the individual; that only private charity and local organizations could reach out to help people in need.

Franklin Roosevelt, like Hoover, was also a fiscal conservative, promising in the 1932 campaign to cut expenditures and to balance the budget. Indeed, in a speech in Pittsburgh he attacked Hoover for not balancing the budget more quickly. But once he got into office, with the suffering of the poor, the elderly, and the unemployed at such devastating levels, he decided he had to revise his economic orthodoxy. He eventually adopted the Keynesian theory that the government could prime the economic pump by increasing spending, by creating jobs and thus stimulating private spending, by being willing to unbalance the budget further. That, of course, led to his famous hundred days, which would go down as the most remarkable use in history of the president's powers to enact sweeping new programs. Acting as a legislative leader, he restructured the relationship of the American government to its people in a permanent way.

He began, of course, with his famous inaugural. We all remember the phrase, "There is nothing to fear but fear itself." But it was much more than that: the attitude of hope he projected; the promise of bold, decisive action; the image of leadership. By making that single speech, he renewed hope and courage and faith on the part of the American people. It's one of the mysteries of leadership the way a successful leader can affect the feelings, the confidence of millions of people. "WE HAVE A LEADER," headlines declared in one newspaper after another.

In those first hundred days, Roosevelt reformed the national banking system, regulated the stock market, and created the Civilian Conservation Corps to employ unemployed youths in conservation efforts. He later set up the Works Progress Administration to put people to work all over the country. He put government in the business of refinancing homes and farm mortgages so that people wouldn't lose their homes, and he established a welfare system for those who could not work. Ever since, those hundred days have been a certain measuring mark for new presidents—and not happily for many, who understandably don't want to be measured against those unusual times.

Many of Roosevelt's programs were only temporary so-
lutions to the problems of the Depression. When the war
came, bringing an end to unemployment, the Public
Works Administration, the National Youth Administration,
the CCC were no longer needed. But other programs have
remained permanent parts of our governmental landscape: Social Security; government regulation of the stock
market through the Securities and Exchange Commission;
federal credit assistance to home buyers, small businesses,
and farmers; federal protection of labor's right to orga-
nize; the minimum wage.

Roosevelt recognized when he came to run for president the second time in 1936 that he was vulnerable to Republican attacks for not keeping his bold promise to
balance the budget. He particularly worried about that
speech he had made in Pittsburgh, where he criticized
Hoover. So he called a White House staff meeting to figure
out his response to the inevitable Republican attacks.
"Well, boss," one of his aides said, "there's only one answer. Simply deny that you ever set foot in Pittsburgh in
your entire life."

At the Democratic Convention in 1936, Roosevelt answered the attacks in dramatic form. He admitted he had
not kept his pledge. He admitted that he had made some
mistakes in the early years. But then he quoted the famous
line: "Better," he said, "the occasional faults of a govern-

ment guided by a spirit of charity and compassion than the constant omissions of a government frozen in the ice of its own indifference."

As he was making his way up to the podium to that "Rendezvous with Destiny" speech, leaning on the arms of his son and a Secret Service agent, his braces locked in place to make it seem as if he could walk (he really could not on his own power), he reached over to shake the hand of a poet. He immediately lost his balance and fell to the floor, his braces unlocked, his speech sprawled about him. He said to the people around him, "Get me up in shape." They dusted him off, picked him up almost like a rag doll, put his braces back in place, and helped him up to the podium. He then somehow managed to deliver that extraordinary speech.

Perhaps even more extraordinary, there was then an unspoken code on the part of the press never to photograph him in his wheelchair, never to show him on his crutches, certainly never to show him sprawled, broken, on the floor. So reporters never mentioned that he had fallen. They simply focused on the words of the speech that he delivered.

In addition to expanding the use of the president's legislative powers, Roosevelt made innovative use of the president's role as chief executive. He was trying to administer all these new programs in the face of a conservative bureaucracy staffed with holdovers from previous administrations, and he feared the New Deal programs would be sabotaged. So on top of the old agencies, he established a whole series of new agencies committed to his programs, which at times led to disorderliness and chaos. But it kept the government moving forward and brought thousands of energetic, idealistic people to Washington to carry out his goals.

Eventually, he called on the Congress to enlarge the president's staff to provide leadership over this vast apparatus. In 1939 a law created the Executive Office of the Presidency, a minibureaucracy that greatly expanded the modern presidency to include eventually the Council of Economic Advisers, the National Security Council, and the Office of Management and Budget. The president, after this moment, was no longer a person but an institution.

Central to all of his success and power was an extraordinary link that he established between the presidency and the American people by three means. First, he grasped the mantle of party leadership, remaking the Democrats into a majority party comprising working-class Americans, immigrants, southerners, and blacks. Second, he held press conferences twice a week. Previous press conferences had been staid affairs where reporters had to ask written questions, but Roosevelt took oral questions and answered spontaneously—with such zest that reporters couldn't wait for his appearances.

Third, and most important, he broadcast the remarkable series of "fireside chats." Each president must find the means of communication that fits his own skills and the technology of the times. In Abraham Lincoln's era, it was often four- to eight-hour speeches on picnic grounds; people then were entertained by public leaders speaking that long. Lincoln also used his exceptional writing skill to produce long letters to newspapers, which were then reprinted in pamphlet form. Today the main medium is television. Eventually, it may be the Internet. But in Roosevelt's time, radio had come into its own as the means of mass communication.

He delivered only thirty fireside chats in his entire twelve years as president, which meant only two or three a year. He understood something our modern presidents do not: that less is more, and that if you go before the public only when you have something dramatic to say, something they need to hear, they will listen. Indeed, over 80 percent of the adult radio audience consistently listened to his fireside chats.

The novelist Saul Bellow, in a wonderful passage, wrote that so many people listened to Roosevelt's fireside chats sitting in their kitchens and parlors that if you walked down the street on a hot Chicago night and the windows were open, you could keep walking down the street and not miss a word of what Roosevelt was saying. And what mattered was not simply Roosevelt's voice but the awareness that everyone else was listening at the same time. You felt connected, somehow, to your fellow Americans. When a leader is able in a democracy to create that sense of connection among the people at large, it may be his greatest source of power.

Now to be sure, not everybody was happy listening to Roosevelt. Some Republicans felt that he was a traitor to his own wealthy class. And I've heard people say their fathers actually threw the radios against the wall and forbade their families ever to listen to "that man in the White House," as they called him. But he willingly accepted the hatred of a small minority so long as the majority of Americans felt that he was on their side. It is a fact that sometimes presidents can court enemies—so long as it's policy-driven and policy-based—and in doing so help clarify the process. That is very different from the recent Clinton scandal, where the enemies' antipathy often seemed based less on policy than on a cultural divide or even a visceral hatred of the president. The salutary effect of controversy-producing policy debates seems to be missing.

Although the role the president played in carrying the American people through the Great Depression deserves lasting praise, it took the war to bring an end to that depression. So perhaps an even greater part of Roosevelt's legacy relates to his use of the role of commander in chief in the years before and during World War II.

In the spring of 1940, Germany had conquered all of Western Europe, leaving Great Britain standing alone against the Nazi juggernaut. Britain desperately needed America's help to survive; it was predicted that the Nazis were ready to invade Britain at any moment. But Roosevelt was hindered in two significant ways. First, the country was profoundly isolationist. Congress had passed a series of laws that tightly restrained the president's war powers, laws deliberately designed to keep the United States out of conflicts in Europe and forbidding the shipment of arms to any belligerent nation. And second, the U.S. military establishment had so collapsed after World War I that we had almost no modern tanks, weapons, or planes, in contrast to Germany, which had spent a decade building its military might.

In fact, America in 1940 stood only eighteenth in military power. The country's military leaders warned Roosevelt that even if he could figure out a way to send the limited weapons that we did have to Britain, it could be disastrous. If Britain fell to Germany, as was predicted would happen in six months, and if Germany then turned against the United States and used our captured weapons against our boys, Roosevelt would be impeached—or worse, one military leader predicted: hanged from a lamppost for sending to Britain the supplies our boys needed.

But Roosevelt made the bold decision that unless America helped Britain survive, all of Western civilization was at risk. And he was willing to risk his presidency. In secret dealings with Winston Churchill, knowing that the Senate would never ratify a treaty, he worked out an executive agreement by which Britain would receive fifty over-aged destroyers in return for America's right to lease a series of British bases all around the world. The trade seemed, on the surface, to violate the neutrality acts. But Roosevelt's attorney general argued that it was legal because under a newly expanded definition of commander in chief Roosevelt had authority to dispose of the armed forces in any way he chose as long as it increased the security of the nation. And in this amazing deal, where he got ninety-nine-year leases on these bases, worth far more than fifty old destroyers, he could argue that he had added to the national security.

When Churchill ran out of money to pay for these American weapons a few months later, Roosevelt himself came up with the idea of lend-lease—a gentlemen's agreement, he said, to eliminate the dollar sign, to lend our weapons to Britain and then get them back when they were no longer needed. It didn't really make much sense.

A lot of these weapons were not going to come back in working order. But he made his point come alive to the American people with his homely analogy: "If your neighbor's house is on fire, you will lend your hose to put that fire out knowing it will save not only the neighbor's house but your own, and then you can get the hose back when the fire is gone."

And somehow, through his ability to communicate, he educated and molded public opinion. At the start of this process, the people were wholly against the idea of any involvement with Britain. By the time the debate finished in the Congress and the Lend-Lease Act was passed, the majority opinion in the country was for the lend-lease program. That is what presidential leadership should and must be about. Not reflecting public opinion polls, taking focus groups to figure out what the people are thinking at that moment, and then simply telling them what they're thinking, but rather moving the nation forward to where you believe its collective energy needs to go.

At the same time Roosevelt moved the American people from isolationism to a greater understanding of the Allied cause, he began the unparalleled process of mobilizing war production to catch up with Germany. Though his relations with the business community had been anything but warm in the 1930s, he recognized that he had to change his tack. He had to reach out to business and form a new partnership because the government couldn't build the ships, the tanks, and the weapons; only business could. So he brought in leading businessmen to run the production agencies. They were filled with patriotic fervor even before we were part of the war, and they did an extraordinary job.

And then he inspired the American people when he told them to put their mattresses on top of their cars and move to those cities where the war plants were being built. Suddenly, in vacant fields and open lots, whole industries were coming to life. And then he got Congress to allow business to write off the cost of construction and investment, exempt business from antitrust laws, and guarantee profits on the government contracts.

This unparalleled partnership with business was not forged at the expense of labor. Roosevelt insisted on high wages. He insisted on overtime pay, new fringe benefits, expanded union membership, and a progressive tax code, so, as he said, the workers would have their own desire to fulfill their part of this production bargain.

And though Roosevelt ever after has been seen as the symbol of big government and the controlled economy, that partnership with private enterprise was the most productive in all of American history. By 1943 we had not only caught up with Germany in our production of weapons, tanks, and planes, but we were outproducing all of the Axis powers and all the Allied powers combined, so that our weapons were being used by our allies in all the four corners of the world: 300,000 planes, 100,000 tanks, 2 million trucks. The production figures were so astronomical that one historian said it was equivalent to building two Panama Canals every month. And through it all Roosevelt continued to speak to the American people, rallying their energies.

My favorite of his fireside chats took place after the war had begun. He knew it was time to bolster people's morale because we were losing battles in the Pacific. So he asked everyone in the country to get a map and spread it out so that he could go over these battles with them. The man who ran C. S. Hammond's map store in New York said he had never sold as many maps as he sold that single week. That night Roosevelt started out very soberly, telling the American people that it would take many months before the tide of the war would turn because we were still in the infancy of this production battle. Unlike later presidents in the Vietnam War, who promised light at the end of the tunnel and failed to gird the people for the length of the war, Roosevelt was always honest about how long it would take before we would even see victories.

But after that sober beginning, he evinced absolute confidence that eventually this war would be won because a democracy releases the free energies of a free people in a manner that not even the most efficient dictatorship ever can. And he brought his point to life by running through American history. Presidents in the olden days used to call on American history to engage us more readily than they do now.

He recalled the extreme hardships at Valley Forge, when George Washington's troops were running out of supplies and it seemed that all was lost. But they persevered, and the revolution was won. He recounted the days of the pioneers going over the Rocky Mountains, the early days of the Civil War, the industrial revolution. It was so powerful that thousands of telegrams came into the White House telling him, "You've got to go on the radio every day. It's the only way morale will be sustained." But he wrote back with knowing insight, saying, "If my speeches ever become routine, if I am overexposed, they will lose their effectiveness."

I think perhaps no figure appreciated more fully the role Roosevelt's confidence played during the war than his great friend and ally Winston Churchill. "To encounter Roosevelt," Churchill once said with his remarkable facility with words, "with all of his buoyant sparkle, his iridescent personality, and his sublime confidence, was like opening your first bottle of champagne—an absolutely unforgettable experience."

It turned out that Churchill was in a position to know

about Roosevelt, for he spent weeks and months at a time living in the White House in a room diagonally across from Roosevelt's during World War II. He became a part of an intimate circle of friends who were also living in the family quarters of the White House during the war, including Franklin's secretary, Missy Lehand, who had started working for him in 1920, loved him the rest of her life, and was his hostess when Eleanor was on the road; Franklin's closest adviser, Harry Hopkins, who came one night for dinner, slept over, and didn't leave until the war was coming to an end; Eleanor's closest friend, a former reporter named Lorena Hickock; and a beautiful princess from Norway, in exile in America during the war, who visited on the weekends.

Just imagine what the modern media would make of the Roosevelt White House. A secretary in love with her boss, a woman reporter in love with Eleanor, a princess visiting on the weekends, Britain's prime minister drinking from the moment he awakened till the moment he went to bed at night. And yet there was then an unwritten rule that the private lives of our public figures were relevant only if they had a direct impact on their leadership. What a wise rule that allowed these unconventional relationships to flourish.

It wasn't a small thing, because these friendships were absolutely essential to Roosevelt. They allowed him to relax and replenish his energies to face the struggles of the following day. Because he was paralyzed from the waist down, he couldn't relax the way other presidents could. He couldn't walk the White House grounds. He couldn't play golf or tennis. Conversation was his main form of relaxation, and having his close associates there twenty-four hours a day meant he could relax at any moment of the day or night.

Roosevelt was also able to relax with ten-day fishing trips in the middle of the war. The press would follow him on a little boat in case there was a press conference or some emergency, but they gave him distance. Indeed, on one of those fishing trips he came up with the whole lend-lease idea. He argued that you had to get away from Washington, away from the conventional wisdom of the moment, to think creatively.

He also relaxed by watching movies. He particularly loved mysteries. He probably would have loved the action movies of today. It was said that the only time he didn't get to see the movies that he liked was when his wife Eleanor chose them, because then he had to sit through *The Grapes of Wrath* or a documentary on civil rights.

And yet despite the major differences in their temperaments—indeed, I would argue, *because* of those differences—Eleanor and Franklin forged their historic partnership, a partnership all the more remarkable since it was born, in many ways, in the pain of Eleanor's discovery in 1918, thirteen years into their marriage, that Franklin was having an affair with a young woman named Lucy Mercer. She came upon a packet of love letters from Lucy to Franklin and later said the bottom dropped out of her world.

But after he pledged never to see Lucy again, she agreed to stay with him in marriage. It reconstituted their relationship, for it gave Eleanor freedom that most married women didn't have then to go outside her marriage to find fulfillment. She immediately became involved in settlement-house work, grew close to a circle of women activists fighting for child labor regulations and a minimum wage, and learned that she had a whole range of talents she never before knew she had: for public speaking, organizing, and articulating a cause.

Then her activism became critical to her husband as well. In 1921, when he contracted polio and became a paraplegic, she became, as he said over and over again in gratitude, his eyes and his ears, traveling first to New York State and then to the entire country on his behalf. She was on the road talking with migrant workers, coal miners, tenant farmers, southern blacks, bringing him back brutally honest reports about which of his New Deal programs were working and which were failing—something leaders all too rarely get from subordinates who don't want to tell them the truth.

Franklin often said of Eleanor that she fought for what *should* be done, whereas he was concerned with what *could* be done, and therein lay the strength of their partnership. Now to be sure, there were flaws on both sides. At times, Roosevelt said, Eleanor had a backbone that simply would not bend. She was so concerned with what should be done that she was insensitive to what could be done, so caught up in her good works that she couldn't relax when he just desperately wanted to sit by her side.

Eleanor was aware of her husband's flaws as well. At times, she said, "He was so skilled in anticipating what others wanted from him that he would seem to nod agreeably at everything everyone said in his office. So everyone left thinking he was agreeing with them when he wasn't at all. Perhaps fewer friends would have been lost by bluntness," she said, "than by the misunderstandings that arose from his charming ambiguity."

At times, too, his arrogance diminished his political instincts, leading him to an unsuccessful attempt to purge his opponents in the 1938 election. And similarly, his arrogance led to an ill-defined court-packing scheme that also failed.

Beyond these temperamental failures, one must concede far more serious failures that led to his incarceration of the Japanese Americans on the basis of a specious assumption that it was necessary for national security, producing one of the most far-reaching civil liberties violations in the history of our country. And also, sadly, the lack of a more decisive response to the problem of the European Jews, both in not opening the doors to more immigration before Hitler shut those doors and in not doing something to bomb the train tracks or the concentration camps themselves once those camps became known.

But in the end Franklin Roosevelt's great strengths far outweighed his weaknesses. His leadership at home kept the American people working together with full energy and commitment through the deadliest war in history. And his leadership abroad kept the Allies working together on the side of freedom until a great victory was achieved that preserved Western civilization from the yoke of Nazi tyranny.

During the war Roosevelt suffered a series of losses. His secretary, Missy Lehand, had a stroke when she was only forty and was never able to speak intelligibly again. His mother, Sarah Delano Roosevelt, died at Hyde Park. He was so lonely that he turned to Eleanor and asked her to be his wife again, his companion, to stop traveling. But although she promised to stay home more often, she was drawn almost as a magnet to the road. Eventually he brought their daughter, Anna, to be the hostess at the White House that Missy Lehand had once been.

In the last year of his life, as the president's health declined, he resumed—with Anna's help—his friendship with Lucy Mercer. Lucy was with him at Warm Springs, Georgia, when Roosevelt collapsed and died. She knew enough to leave immediately, but when Eleanor flew down later that night, she discovered the truth. I can hardly comprehend the dignity Eleanor mustered to take that famous train trip from Warm Springs to Washington, never letting the world outside, gathered by the hundreds of thousands to mourn their beloved leader, know the hurt she was feeling inside.

Later that summer Eleanor began traveling the country again. Everywhere she went people told her how much they loved her husband. Porters, taxicab drivers, elevator operators told her how much better their lives were as a result of his leadership. Blacks shared the sense of mastery they felt in the jobs they performed, the courage they had shown on the battlefield. Women spoke of the new independence they had found during the war, the pleasure and the sociability of the workplace.

Eleanor talked to veterans who were going to college on Roosevelt's GI Bill of Rights, the majority of whom would never have had the opportunity for higher education without this generous piece of legislation. She talked to union leaders and laboring men and saw that unions were stronger than ever before.

She realized, she later said, that the war had become a vehicle for social reform in more ways than she ever could have dreamed; that the country had been transformed from a pyramidal society, with only a few people at the top enjoying the wealth of the country, and the majority at the bottom. Now a giant middle class had been formed. And as she absorbed the extent of all these positive changes, she began to feel, in a somewhat romantic metaphor, as if a giant transference of energy had taken place.

As Eleanor described it, at the start of the war, Roosevelt was strong, vital, productive. The country was weak, isolationist, unprepared for war. But gradually he had projected his strength onto the American people so that they got stronger and stronger while he was weakened. In the end he had died. But the country he left behind had emerged more powerful, more productive, and more socially just than ever before.

With this image in her mind, Eleanor was able to reach deep within herself and forgive Franklin for resuming his friendship with Lucy Mercer in the last year of his life. And she was able to forgive their daughter, Anna, as well. It was a reconciliation that allowed Eleanor to go forward without bitterness, remembering only the best of times in her marriage, drawing strength from her husband's memory.

It is possible to look at Franklin Roosevelt from the outside in, as the media might today, and to accuse him of infidelity for resuming his friendship with Lucy Mercer, even of harassment for his close relationship with his secretary, Missy Lehand. But these labels would totally miss the mark.

For I believe the challenge in writing history today is to resist the modern tendency—the tendency to label, to stereotype, to expose, to denigrate—and instead, to bring empathy to our subjects so that the past can truly come alive, even if just for a few moments, in all its beauty, sorrow, and glory.

CHAPTER THREE

DWIGHT D. EISENHOWER AND JOHN F. KENNEDY

A STUDY IN CONTRASTS

BY MICHAEL R. BESCHLOSS

★

For most of American history, the presidency has been a weak office—and that was very much in keeping with what the framers intended. They did not want another king of England; they didn't want a dictator. They made sure that there were checks against presidential power, one of them being impeachment, and they were very worried about the idea of a president who would do too much. So a lot of the power of the presidency comes not at all from what's in the Constitution but from two other factors.

The first is the president's ability to go to the American people and ask them for something—especially sacrifice. One very good example would be Franklin Roosevelt in 1940, saying, "You may not want to get prepared for a possible war in Europe and Asia, but this is something I've thought a lot about and this is a sacrifice that we may have to make." Another example would be a president's appeal for a painful tax increase to achieve a balanced budget.

The second source of presidential power is a president's ability to get things out of Congress. The founders hoped that presidents would have such moral authority and people would think they were so wise that members of

Congress would be intimidated. If a president went to Congress and asked for something like civil rights, members would take heed. That's one reason why Lyndon Johnson was a much more powerful president in 1964, 1965, and 1966 than I think others might have been: Because of his experience as one of the most canny and powerful leaders in the history of Congress, he was extraordinarily effective at getting what he wanted.

For most of our lifetimes, we have been in a situation that is something of an aberration. When I was ten years old, hoping to be able to write history about presidents when I grew up, it seemed very glamorous. I thought these people were, to crib a phrase from Leonardo DiCaprio, "kings of the world." The president was the centerpiece of the American political solar system, the center of our foreign and domestic policy, the most powerful person in the American government—and America was astride the world. That was the case from Franklin Roosevelt until the last year of George Bush.

In the 1930s Congress and the American people granted Roosevelt extraordinary influence over domestic affairs. In the wake of Pearl Harbor, they extended that power into foreign affairs. After 1945, Americans thought it was a good idea for power to flow to Washington. That enhanced the power of presidents. People liked federal action and federal programs. Congress was inclined to defer to the chief executive in foreign policy because we had to win the cold war. Then in the late 1960s and early 1970s, Americans grew more skeptical about Big Government. Power began to flow away from Washington. Then the cold war ended, and foreign policy seemed less urgent. The result is that now we are returning to a moment in which presidents don't have the kind of power that they had between the 1930s and the 1980s.

Dwight Eisenhower became president of the United States in 1953, at the apex of presidential power. But that power was enhanced by the man himself and the situation in which he found himself. It is hard to imagine a leader in a more commanding position. As the hero of World War II in Europe, Eisenhower enjoyed as august a national and world reputation as anyone who has ever entered the White House. With his impeccable reputation for character and integrity, he was as much a national father figure as George Washington.

Eisenhower had been elected by a landslide, and in that election he took both houses of Congress back from the Democrats. He could fairly argue that his ample coattails had made the difference. This was a new president with enormous reservoirs of political strength but also limited ambitions—much more limited than those of Woodrow Wilson, Franklin Roosevelt, or Lyndon Johnson.

Although he would never have alienated conservatives

in his party by saying so in public, Eisenhower had no desire to turn back the clock on the New Deal. Instead, he wanted to consolidate those reforms and do what Republicans do: Administer the programs more efficiently and economically. Beyond that he saw himself—among the conflicting demands of labor, business, finance, and other engines of the American economy—as a balance wheel poised to let postwar prosperity roar ahead under a balanced budget.

He wanted to eliminate isolationism from the Republican Party and postwar America. We sometimes forget how close Republicans came to nominating the isolationist senator Robert Taft of Ohio in 1952. Ike had such deep convictions about this issue that in the winter of 1952 he went to Taft and said, "I feel so strongly about defending the Free World against the Soviets that I will make you a deal. If you renounce isolationism, I won't run against you for president."

Taft easily could have accepted, and Eisenhower never would have been president. It shows you how deeply he felt about this. He wanted to use his office to make sure that no postwar national leader could come to power without vowing to ensure that the United States would remain permanently engaged in the world. That comes about as close as anything Eisenhower had to a deep political conviction.

He hoped that by the end of his eight years in office he

would be able somehow to reduce the harshness of the cold war. As a military man, he knew the danger of nuclear war. Once, sitting through a briefing by a civil defense official who was blithely describing how the federal government could survive underground after a Soviet nuclear attack, Ike told him to stop. "We won't be carrying on with government," he barked. "We'll be grubbing for worms!" He was disgusted that the United States had to spend billions of dollars on what he called "sterile" military programs, when it could have invested in schools and hospitals and roads.

To hold down the arms race as much as possible, he worked out a wonderful tacit agreement with Soviet premier Nikita Khrushchev. Khrushchev wanted to build up his economy. He didn't want to spend a lot of money on the Soviet military because he wanted to start feeding people and recover from the devastation of World War II. But he knew that to cover this he would have to give speeches in public that said quite the opposite. So Khrushchev would deliver himself of such memorable lines as, "We Soviets are cranking out missiles like sausages, and we will bury you because our defense structure is pulling ahead of the United States."

Eisenhower dealt with this much as an adult deals with a small boy who is lightly punching him in the stomach. He figured that leaving Khrushchev's boasts unanswered was a pretty small price to pay if it meant that Khrushchev would not spend much money building up his military.

The result was that the arms race was about as slow during the 1950s as it could have been, and Eisenhower was well on the way to creating an atmosphere of communication. Had the U-2 not fallen down in 1960 and had the presidential campaign taken place in a more peaceful atmosphere, I think you would have seen John Kennedy and Richard Nixon competing on the basis of who could increase the opening to the Soviets that Eisenhower had created. Whether or not that would have sped the end of the cold war is open to argument.

In 1953 Eisenhower was disheartened by the bitterness and exhaustion in the American political climate. We had been through a stock market crash, a Great Depression, five years of global war, a growing Soviet threat, full-fledged cold war, the Korean War, McCarthyism and the backlash against it—all in the space of less than a generation. Our nerves were frayed. Ike wanted to be the calming, unifying national symbol who could give us a little bit of breathing space.

What personal qualities did Eisenhower bring to the Oval Office? The most obvious: He was the most popular human being in America and probably the most popular human being in the world. But he was also a much more intelligent man than people understood at the time.

People who watched his press conferences—filled with those sentences that lacked verbs and never seemed to end—thought Ike was a wonderful guy but not too bright. Now, almost a half-century later, we have access to his letters and diaries and records of his private meetings. When you take Ike off the public platform and put him in a small room where he's talking candidly to his aides and friends, you find a leader much in command of complex issues—very different from the caricature of the time.

Harry Truman once predicted that when Ike became president he would be frustrated. Truman said that as a general, Eisenhower would shout, "Do this!" and "Do that!"—but that in the White House, when he did that, nothing would happen. Indeed, Ike had never been in domestic politics. But what people overlooked was that in the army for almost forty years he had been operating in large, bureaucratic organizations, not least the Allied Expeditionary Force in Europe. This was good experience for a president who had to deal with a rapidly growing CIA and Pentagon—and with ballooning domestic bureaucracies like the new Department of Health, Education, and Welfare.

What qualities did Eisenhower lack? Well, as an orator, he was no Franklin Roosevelt. He seemed to design his language to make sure that no one would remember—or in some cases, understand—what he said. Some scholars, like Fred Greenstein of Princeton, think that Eisenhower was often deliberately boring or opaque as a ploy, to keep from polarizing people. Maybe so, but the inability to use what Theodore Roosevelt called the "bully pulpit" is a big problem for a president. I think it robbed Eisenhower of considerable power that, used in the right way, could have been very important for this country.

Imagine if Eisenhower had been president in 1939. That was when FDR was making the case to the American people that we had to build our own defense forces because we might have to fight a war. His oratorical skills helped to move opinion in Congress and among the American people enough so that when war came, we were prepared. Had Roosevelt been mute, we would have lost World War II.

The ability to move a nation is essential if a president wants to ask Congress and the American people for something. It is just as essential if things are going bad. That's when a president needs to reassure the public. In 1958 America was plunging into recession. Eisenhower refused to improve things by unbalancing the budget. The Republicans lost badly in the 1958 midterm elections, largely because Ike could not or would not explain to Americans why it was necessary to stay the economic course. He allowed his critics to take the initiative, saying, "Eisenhower is tired and washed up and so obsessed with a balanced budget that he doesn't care about people who are suffering."

Another example came the previous year, with the Soviet launching of Sputnik, the first earth satellite. Eisenhower's foes said, "Ike is so lazy and asleep at the switch that he's allowed the Russians to be first to launch a satellite. Now the Russians can drop nuclear weapons on Chicago or Detroit—or Hanover, New Hampshire." In fact, sending up Sputnik was not the same thing as being able to drop a bomb precisely on a target by missile. The Soviets were still years away from being able to do that. But Eisenhower was unable to make that case to the American people. The result was near national hysteria.

Another of Ike's shortcomings was as a horse trader. He once said, "I don't know how to do what you have to do to get something out of a congressman." You wouldn't have heard Lyndon Johnson saying such a thing. Getting members of Congress to do things they don't want to do is a crucial part of being president.

On one of the tapes LBJ made of his private conversations as president, you hear Johnson in 1964. He knows that the key to getting his civil rights bill passed will be Everett Dirksen of Illinois, Republican leader of the Senate. He calls Dirksen, whom he's known for twenty years, and essentially says, "Ev, I know you have some doubts about this bill, but if you decide to support it, a hundred years from now every American schoolchild will know two names—Abraham Lincoln and Everett Dirksen." Dirksen liked the sound of that. He supported the bill, and the rest was history. You will never find an example of a conversation like that in the annals of Dwight Eisenhower. And his diffidence about Congress limited his ability to get things done.

If Eisenhower were president in a time requiring a leader standing in the epicenter of heroic change—like Roosevelt in the 1930s and 1940s, for example—he probably would have been a disaster because he lacked the ambitions and the skills that kind of presidential leadership requires. Yet Eisenhower was magnificently suited to the 1950s. He got people to accept Social Security and other controversial reforms as a permanent way of American life. For much of the decade, he balanced the budget, kept inflation low, and presided over a postwar boom. He fathered the interstate highway system. He was the very image of a chief of state. He made Americans feel happy about themselves and their country. He killed isolationism. He muted the U.S.–Soviet arms race as much as any president could have.

To use the parlance of West Point, I'd suggest three demerits in Ike's record as president. The first: Joseph McCarthy. Eisenhower was a civil libertarian. He knew what Senator McCarthy's reckless charges about internal communism were doing to this country. Imagine if Eisenhower had stood up in 1953 and said, "McCarthyism is a poison in this society. Believe me, of all people, I'll be the last to let this country be injured by communists within, but we can't tear this nation apart." That could have changed history. Instead, Ike was stunningly quiet, although some recent revisionists argue that he tried to tunnel against McCarthy behind the scenes.

The most coherent statement Ike made against McCarthy was at Dartmouth in June 1953. He had been chatting about the virtues of playing golf. He urged Dartmouth men to have fun in their lives. They didn't seem to need the advice. But toward the end of that speech, he got serious. He had been told how McCarthy's agents had tried to have certain "subversive" books removed from U.S. embassy libraries abroad. He told the Dartmouth graduates, "Don't join the book burners. Instead, go to the library and read books on communism so you'll know what you're fighting against." Nicely said, but these two paragraphs got little attention. They leave you feeling that Eisenhower could and should have said so much more.

Demerit two: civil rights. Ike never understood how vital it was to integrate American society after World War II. Imagine how he could have used that great moral authority and world reputation. He could have said in 1953,

"I went to Europe and helped win the Second World War, but that was just part of the job. Now we have to finish what we fought for by bringing equal rights to all Americans." No other political figure would have carried so much weight.

But Ike had something of a blind spot on civil rights. He had spent a lot of his life in the South and, I think, overestimated the degree of resistance to a civil rights bill. We now know that in 1954, when the Supreme Court in *Brown v. Board of Education* ordered the desegregation of public schools, Eisenhower privately thought it a bad idea.

Ike had an aide named Frederic Morrow, who was the first African American to serve on a president's staff. Morrow would talk to the president about civil rights on occasion and would come away feeling that he had made some headway. Then Ike would fly to Georgia for a hunting weekend with southern friends. And when he came back, it was almost as if his conversation with Morrow had never occurred.

Civil rights was a case where Eisenhower's instincts of compromise and moderation served him badly. Segregation was a moral issue. I think that the president's foot-dragging caused the civil rights revolution, when it reached full force in the 1960s, to be more bitter and violent.

The final demerit: One test of leaders is how they make

sure that their ideas and programs will live on after they're gone. One way they do that is by building a political movement like a political party. Eisenhower tried to recreate his party in the image of what he called "modern Republicanism." But he failed. Four years after he left office, Republicans scorned his moderation as a "dime-store New Deal" and nominated Barry Goldwater. The Republican Party we see today is far more the party of Goldwater than of Eisenhower.

Another way you make sure your policies survive is with your words. But so unable or unwilling was Eisenhower to use his powers of persuasion that some of the basic tenets of his political credo vanished almost as soon as he left the White House. Because Ike failed to make the case for a balanced budget, his Democratic successors were able to start the great inflation of the 1960s. Because Ike failed to make the case for a moderate arms race, John Kennedy started what was at that time the largest arms buildup in human history.

Another way is to make sure you are followed by leaders who will carry on your purposes. Here Eisenhower failed. He once said that one of the biggest disappointments of his life was that in the race to succeed him, John Kennedy defeated his vice president, Richard Nixon. He called that "a repudiation of everything I've stood for for eight years."

DWIGHT D. EISENHOWER AND JOHN F. KENNEDY

It is hard to imagine two more different men than Dwight Eisenhower and John F. Kennedy—and perhaps in no way more so than this: Eisenhower in 1953 had access to vast amounts of power; Kennedy in 1961 had access to little.

Kennedy had been elected president by a margin of only 100,000 votes. Congress remained Democratic, but since most members had run well ahead of the new president, they felt they owed him little. As Kennedy saw it, he was faced by a House and Senate dominated by hostile coalitions of conservative Republicans and southern Democrats. Many of those who had known him as a fellow congressman or senator found it hard to get out of the habit of thinking of him as a distracted, absentee backbencher.

The American people had voted for Kennedy—narrowly—but they didn't really know him. Unlike Eisenhower, from the moment he was elected, Kennedy had to work hard to make an impression. He was always worried that he looked too young for people to think of him as a president. And when you look at videotape and newsreels of the period, you notice how stiff and formal Kennedy is on the platform.

JFK came to the presidency devoid of executive experience. The biggest organizations he had ever run were his Senate office and the PT-109 he commanded during World War II. What's more, he had been seeking the presidency for so long that he had only vague instincts about where he wanted to take the country. He did want to do something in civil rights. In the 1960 campaign, he promised to end discrimination "with the stroke of a pen." On health care, education, the minimum wage, and other social issues, he was a mainstream Democrat. He hoped to get the country through eight years without a nuclear holocaust and to improve things with the Soviets, if possible. He wanted a nuclear test ban treaty.

But as he was riding to the inaugural ceremonies with Kennedy in 1961, James Reston, the great *New York Times* columnist, asked what kind of country Kennedy wanted to leave his successor. Kennedy looked at him quizzically, as if he were looking at the man in the moon. Kennedy's method was never the grand vision of a Wilson or Reagan. It was crisis management—hour to hour to hour.

Kennedy's vow to land a man on the moon before 1970 is a perfect example. When he became president, he had no intention of launching a crash moon program. Advisers told him it would be too expensive and would unbalance a space program that was divided among communications, military, weather, exploration, and other projects.

But in the spring of 1961, the Russians injured American pride by launching the first man, Yuri Gagarin, into space. Then Kennedy suffered an embarrassing defeat when he and the CIA tried to use Cuban exiles to invade Cuba at the Bay of Pigs and seize the country from Fidel Castro. In the wake of that botched invasion, he badgered his aides for some quick fix that would help to restore American prestige. The moon-landing program was rolled out of mothballs.

People at the time often said Eisenhower was responsible for the Bay of Pigs, since it was Eisenhower's plan to take Cuba back from Castro. I think that has a hard time surviving scrutiny. Eisenhower would not necessarily have approved the invasion's going forward, and he would not necessarily have run it the same way. His son once asked him, "Is there a possibility that if you had been president, the Bay of Pigs would have happened?" Ike reminded him of Normandy and said, "I don't run no bad invasions."

Unlike Eisenhower, who almost flaunted his affinity for paperback westerns, Kennedy was a voracious reader of high intelligence. And we also remember JFK as one of the great orators of American history, which is only half right. Extemporaneously, he tended to speak too fast and with language that did not last for long. The great utterances we think of as coming from Kennedy—"Ask not what your country can do for you"; "We choose to go to the moon"; "*Ich bin ein Berliner*"—were almost all in prepared speeches, usually written by his gifted speechwriter Theodore Sorensen. If you read Kennedy's speeches from his earliest days as a congressman in 1947, you can see the difference at the instant Sorensen signs on in 1953. It's almost like the moment in *The Wizard of Oz* when the film goes from black and white to color. Suddenly, Kennedy had found his voice.

And when he used that voice, he was amazingly successful in moving public opinion. Think of the impact of Kennedy's inaugural or his Oval Office speech in October 1962, announcing Soviet missiles in Cuba and what he planned to do about them, or his civil rights address in June 1963, when he finally declared—as no president had ever declared—that civil rights was a "moral issue" that was "as old as the Scriptures and as clear as the Constitution."

JFK may never have run a large bureaucratic organization, but he was terrific at managing small groups. Look at the paramount moment of the Kennedy presidency—the Cuban missile crisis. How did he deal with the problem? He formed a small group of trusted officials, the Ex Comm (Executive Committee), which met in the Cabinet Room under the close supervision of the president and his brother Robert. Robert Kennedy was probably the most powerful member of a presidential entourage that we've seen in this century. That cut both ways. On the one hand, John Kennedy had someone he could rely upon as absolutely loyal, someone who totally shared his purposes. But on the other hand, it was virtually impossible for the president to distance himself from anything his attorney general did, since people assumed that when Robert Kennedy spoke, the message came from his brother.

The tape recordings of the Ex Comm meetings over thirteen days make it clear how enormously important it was to have Kennedy and his brother massaging the discussion. During the first week, the group moved from an almost certain intention to bomb the missile sites and invade Cuba to what JFK finally did: throw a quarantine around the island and demand that Nikita Khrushchev haul the missiles out. We now know that had Kennedy bombed, it might have easily escalated to a third world war. If Eisenhower had been running those meetings, with his Olympian approach, they might have been not nearly so effective. Here, Kennedy's talent for crisis management may have saved the world.

He had less success in his day-to-day dealings with Congress. One senator observed that the president would call him and say, "I sure hope I can count on your help on this bill." And he'd reply, "Mr. President, I'd love to help you, but it would cause me big problems in my state." If Lyndon Johnson had been president, he would have said, "Tough luck!" and pulled every lever he could to get his bill, even if it meant phoning the senator's bank and having his mortgage called. But Kennedy would say, "I understand. Perhaps you'll be with me the next time."

A good example is civil rights. Whatever he had pledged in the 1960 campaign, he was too overwhelmed by the opposition on Capitol Hill to do much to integrate American society. Voters who remembered his promise to end racial separation with a stroke of his pen angrily sent bottles of ink to the White House. Privately, he kept saying, "Wait until 1965. I've got to get reelected in a big way. If I'm lucky enough to run against Barry Goldwater, I'll win in a landslide with a big margin in Congress. Then on all the legislation I want, I can let 'er rip."

But the "Negro revolution," as people called it then, would not wait. In June 1963, with the South erupting in flames, Kennedy sent Congress a civil rights bill that was radical for its time. It was late, and he was pushed into it by events, but this was genuinely a profile in courage. JFK's public approval ratings dropped about twenty points. Southern states that had helped him win the presidency in 1960 turned against him. When Kennedy went to Texas in November 1963, he was by no means a shoo-in for reelection, and the reason was civil rights.

Unlike Eisenhower, Kennedy never had the eight years he had hoped for. Only two years, ten months, two days.

And he never got that landslide in 1964. That went to Lyndon Johnson, who did have the good luck to run against Barry Goldwater. Thus to understand JFK's use of power, we have to ask two final questions about what might have happened had he lived.

First, what would have happened to his civil rights bill? I think that there is a good chance the Senate would have defeated it. In the aftermath of Kennedy's murder, Johnson was able to say, "Pass this bill as the memorial to our beloved late president." As I've mentioned, the Johnson tapes show that he used his monumental abilities to squeeze members of Congress to get the bill passed. Had Kennedy lived, neither of those things would have been possible. If you have to pull something redeeming out of the tragedy of Dallas, then, it is fair to say that because JFK gave his life, 20 million African Americans gained their rights sooner than they might have.

The other question is what Kennedy would have done in Vietnam. Some of Kennedy's champions, like Senate majority leader Mike Mansfield and his aide Kenneth O'Donnell, quote him as having said privately that he couldn't pull out before the 1964 election because he would be vilified as soft on communism. According to them, he planned to keep the troops in until after he was safely reelected, get the Saigon government to ask us to leave, and then withdraw.

I tend to be skeptical of this. If true, it means that Kennedy cynically would have kept young Americans in harm's way for fourteen months or more merely to help himself through the next election, then surrendered the commitment for which they'd been fighting.

Nor am I convinced by the notion that a reelected Kennedy in 1965 suddenly would have thrown caution to the winds. He still would have to serve as president for four years, and if he seemed to cave in on Vietnam in those times in which most Americans believed in the domino theory, there would have been a national backlash that would have undercut his ability to get anything he wanted from Congress, foreign or domestic.

And there was always in his mind the possibility that Robert Kennedy, or other Kennedys, might run for president. I doubt that he would have done something that might so injure his family's durability in American politics.

A greater possibility is that if Kennedy had escalated the war for two years and found himself as frustrated as Lyndon Johnson was, he might have been more willing than LBJ to pull out. Throughout his political career, Kennedy was adept at cutting losses.

The fact is, we will never know.

CHAPTER FOUR

LYNDON B. JOHNSON

THE RACE FOR POWER

★

BY ROBERT A. CARO

★

I have never been interested in writing a biography just to tell the life of a famous man. I always wanted to use biography as a means of illuminating the times in which my subjects lived and the great forces that shaped those times, particularly the force that is political power.

In order for this theory of biography to work, of course, you have to find the right man, and I think Lyndon Johnson was the right man, the right prism, if you will, through which to examine national power: first, because he understood it and all its ramifications so well; second, because his use of political power did so much to shape the lives of all Americans.

This understanding of power was evident throughout his adult life, of course. When Lyndon Johnson was in the Senate, during the 1950s, the Senate was dominated, as it had always been, by the seniority system. For their first few years there, young senators weren't even supposed to speak on the floor very often, much less participate in the Senate's inner workings. Even so, just four years after he arrived, Lyndon Johnson was the Democratic leader in the Senate. And having obtained power so quickly, he used it—*very* quickly. In four more years, he succeeded in ramming through the Senate the first civil rights bill to be passed in almost a century.

In those days the Senate was completely dominated by the South. There were fourteen great standing committees of the Senate. Southerners were chairmen of eight of them. They all had the power to speak in the Senate, and they were determined that this civil rights bill would not pass. They had stopped civil rights bills decade after decade.

To watch Johnson get that bill through in 1957 was to see legislative genius. In Britain, where they had Disraeli and Gladstone, they know much more about legislative genius. But in the United States, when we think of political genius we tend to mean executive genius, administrative genius. Lyndon Johnson had legislative genius, and as majority leader of the Senate he turned that institution into something it hadn't been for a century.

In the face of that massed power of the South, in the face of these senators who had vowed that civil rights legislation was never going to pass, Lyndon Johnson got civil rights legislation passed. How did he do it?

Here's just one incident. The southerners were insisting that anyone accused under a voting rights act must get a jury trial; that meant, effectively, that no one in the South would ever be convicted of a voting rights offense. The liberals, of course, could not allow that. George Reedy, one of

Johnson's assistants, says he thought he had finally seen the irresistible force meet the immovable object. There were tremendous fights in the Senate. Then Johnson noticed a southwestern liberal, Clinton Anderson, sitting at his desk writing something. Johnson asked what it was. And Anderson replied, "I think I thought of an amendment that will handle this."

Johnson, the legislative genius, thought Anderson was right—that the amendment would break the impasse—but he knew that if it were introduced by a Democratic liberal, it would never attract the necessary support. So he told Anderson to find a Republican who would cosponsor the measure. Anderson did, and the amendment passed. That was just one of about a hundred logjams Johnson had to break.

Johnson's understanding and use of power had its most far-reaching effects during his presidency. I call his a "watershed presidency." And I use that term in its exact meaning. A watershed is a divide like the Continental Divide. On one side the waters run in one direction; on the other side they run the opposite way. That was Lyndon Johnson's presidency—a true watershed. Its five years were filled with the legislative embodiments of the cause of social justice. Great strides were made toward ending discrimination in public accommodations, in employment, in private housing. Laws of which liberals had dreamed for decades were passed during those five years. Sixty-one separate education laws were passed, as well as laws that provided medical care for the aged and the poor. And, of course—most important of all, in my opinion—there were the civil rights laws, most significantly the voting rights law.

Abraham Lincoln freed black Americans, but it was Lyndon Johnson who led them into the voting booths and put their hands on the levers that gave them control of their own destiny and made them, at last and forever, a part of American political life. He empowered them. The presidency of Lyndon Johnson marked the legislative realization of so many of the liberal aspirations of the twentieth century. His presidency was in many ways the high-water mark of the tides of social justice in the century.

But that, of course, was not the whole story of his presidency. It was also the presidency of the escalation of the Vietnam War. When he came to office, there were 16,000 Americans serving in Vietnam, and they were serving as advisers. By the time he left office, there were 549,000 Americans in Vietnam, and they were in active combat.

As time passes, the true dimensions of the human cost of the Vietnam War become more and more evident because we keep finding out about the numbers of casualties in North Vietnam and South Vietnam. The memorial wall in Washington bears the names of 58,000 Vietnam dead. Those are the dead. The wall does not record the names of Americans who lost limbs or were blinded or were in other ways seriously wounded. If it included the names of the wounded, the wall would have had to be much bigger: The number of Americans who were wounded was 288,000. And those are just the Americans. There were hundreds of thousands of North Vietnamese and South Vietnamese casualties.

"We Shall Overcome." "Hey! Hey! LBJ! How many kids did you kill today?" The War on Poverty. Vietnam. The Great Society. The credibility gap. The presidency—thirty-sixth in the history of the republic—of Lyndon Baines Johnson was a watershed presidency, one of the great divides in American history, in the evolution of the country's policies, both foreign and domestic, and of its image, both in the eyes of the world and in its own eyes.

We can see the seeds of all this—the genius in the acquisition of power, the use and misuse of that power once he had it—in the young Lyndon Johnson.

Franklin D. Roosevelt became acquainted with him in 1937, when Johnson, who was only twenty-eight years old at the time, was elected to Congress. He had run on a platform that emphasized a single word: "Roosevelt." "Roosevelt, Roosevelt, Roosevelt. I'm 100 percent for Roosevelt." That was his campaign slogan.

Almost immediately after Johnson arrived in Washington, a rather remarkable thing happened. Franklin Roosevelt didn't believe in becoming chummy with congressmen. He might spend time with congressional leaders, but he kept the rest of them at a distance. He certainly didn't have much to do with most young freshman congressmen, and Johnson was one of the youngest. But almost immediately after Johnson arrived in Washington, he began to get invited to the White House.

Lyndon Johnson was a gangling young man, six foot three and a half and incredibly thin. He didn't know how to dress. His arms were long, and his jackets and shirts were too short, so his wrists always stuck out. He looked unsophisticated. But it was this young man—not the other congressmen—who was being invited to the White House. At first he would be invited for lunch. Then Roosevelt started inviting him to breakfast. Roosevelt would be having breakfast in bed, sitting up with his cape around his shoulders, and Johnson would be there. Then Roosevelt started inviting Johnson for drinks in the late afternoon, and sometimes, because FDR was a rather lonely president, he would invite Johnson over late in the evening.

Trying to understand why this relationship developed, I asked some of Roosevelt's assistants. One of them, Jim Rowe, said to me, "You have to understand: Franklin Roosevelt was a political genius. When he talked about politics, he was talking at a level at which very few people could follow him and understand what he was really saying. But from the first time that Roosevelt talked to Lyndon Johnson, he saw that Johnson understood *everything* he was talking about."

This young congressman may have been unsophisticated about some things, but about politics—about power—he was sophisticated enough at that early age to understand one of the great masters. Roosevelt was so impressed, in fact, that once he said to Interior Secretary Harold Ickes, "That's the kind of uninhibited young politician I might have been—if only I hadn't gone to Harvard." Roosevelt made a prediction, also to Ickes. He said, "You know, in the next generation or two, the balance of power in the United States is going to shift to the South and West, and this kid, Lyndon Johnson, could be the first southern president."

Roosevelt, as it turned out, was right. And if we are to understand that watershed presidency, it is important to understand Lyndon Johnson's youth and early political career. The seeds of so many significant aspects of that presidency—both its bright aspects and its dark—can be found in those early years.

There were obstacles to learning about Johnson's race for power and about the young Lyndon Johnson. Most of the obstacles were put there by Johnson himself, because of what some called his obsession with secrecy. But as I tried to learn about and understand his early years,

perhaps the biggest obstacle was not Johnson but me—
my background, a life spent almost entirely in a city, with
its museums and concerts and crowded streets. Lyndon
Johnson was raised in the Texas Hill Country—and that
was about as different as a place could be from where I
grew up.

When I was working on the first volume of his biography, the Hill Country started right outside Austin and
went on for hundreds of miles. All told, it covers 24,000
square miles, an area big enough to hold all of New England and several other states and still have plenty left over.
It was a vast, empty, lonely place. You could drive for miles
without passing a single car going in either direction, or a
house. The hills seemed to go on forever. The early settlers
called it "the land of false horizons."

I'll never forget the first time I realized how hard it was
going to be for the ultimate city boy to understand Lyndon Johnson. Johnson City, where Johnson grew up, is
about 47 miles outside Austin. I had driven out of Austin
perhaps 40 miles, and I came to what I later learned was
called Round Mountain, the tallest hill around. As I drove
over the top, I had to stop the car and get out and just
look. In front of me was a barren panorama stretching out
as far as I could see. At first I thought that there was not
one human thing in this entire huge valley, and then all of
a sudden, off in the distance, I saw a little huddle of

houses. That was Johnson City. When Lyndon Johnson was growing up, 323 people lived there.

I remember Lyndon Johnson's brother, Sam Houston Johnson, trying to tell me how lonely it was on the Johnson ranch. The ranch was even more isolated than Johnson City, further back in the hills. One corner of the ranch came down next to the rutted dirt track that ran between Austin and Fredricksburg—and Lyndon and Sam Houston would sit for hours on the fence where it came closest to that road, hoping that one rider would come by, or someone in a carriage, one new person for them to talk to.

It was also hard for me to understand the terrible poverty in the Hill Country. There was no money in Johnson City. One of Lyndon's best friends once carried a dozen eggs to Marble Falls, 22 miles over the hills. He had to ride very slowly so they wouldn't break; he carried them in a box in front of him. The ride took all day. And for those eggs he received one dime.

The bright side of Johnson's youth foreshadows the bright side of his presidency: the passage of laws to broaden social justice for Americans, particularly for Americans whose skins are dark. The bright side is very bright, for Lyndon Johnson was a genius at what his Hill Country populist forebears would have defined as the true duty of government: the duty to use the power of the sovereign state to help its people, especially the least fortunate, people not able to help themselves, people who are trying to fight forces too big for them to fight alone. His father, who was an idealistic rural legislator in the Texas legislature, said, "The job of government is to help people who are caught in the tentacles of circumstance."

During my interviews in the Hill Country, I heard over and over some version of the same phrase: "No matter what Lyndon was like, we loved him because he brought the lights." When Johnson became congressman in 1937, there was no electricity in the Hill Country, and by the time he left as congressman in 1948, he had brought electricity there. The significance of that phrase went right over my head for a long time. I understood intellectually that he had brought electricity, but I didn't understand what that meant, what the lives of the people were like without it.

Because there was no electricity, there were no movies and almost no radio. And the lack of electricity caused hardships far beyond that. Take water, for example. The streams dried up there for most of the year, so you had to get water out of wells. The wells in the Hill Country were generally at least 75 feet deep. Every bucket of water—for drinking, for doing the wash, for every purpose—had to be hauled up. The Department of Agriculture determined then that the average farm family used 200 gallons of water a day. That's 73,000 gallons of water—300 tons—a year. And this had to be brought up by hand from the wells, most of it up by the women of the Hill Country.

I asked these women—elderly now—what life had been like without electricity. They would say, "Well, you're a city boy. You don't know how heavy a bucket of water is, do you?" The wells were now unused and covered with boards, but they would push the boards aside. They'd get out an old bucket, often with the rope still attached, and they'd drop it down in the well and say, "Now, pull it up." And of course it was very heavy. They would show me how they put the rope over the windlass and then over their shoulders. They would throw the whole weight of their bodies into it, pulling it step by step while leaning so far that they were almost horizontal. And these farm wives had yokes like cattle yokes so they could carry two buckets of water at a time.

They would say, "Do you see how round-shouldered I am? Do you see how bent I am?" Now in fact I *had* noticed that these women, who were in their sixties or seventies, did seem more stooped than city women of the same age, but I hadn't understood why. One woman said to me, "I swore I wouldn't be bent like my mother, and then I got married, and the babies came, and I had to start bringing in the water, and I knew I would look exactly like my mother."

When Lyndon Johnson became their congressman in

1937, the people of the Hill Country were living lives not out of the twentieth century but out of the Middle Ages. He promised that if they'd elect him, he'd bring them electricity. Well, they elected him, but no one believed he could do that. A dam had been started on the lower Colorado River at one edge of the Hill Country, but it was the Depression, and the companies building the dam were in financial trouble. And even if you somehow got the dam built and created hydroelectric power, how were you going to get it out across those thousands of miles?

When Johnson got to Washington, he became a protégé of Roosevelt and of Roosevelt's advisers, including Thomas Corcoran—Tommy "the Cork" Corcoran. Tommy the Cork told me, "Every time Lyndon would see me, he would ask me to remind Roosevelt about the appropriation for the dam. And I bothered Roosevelt so much that finally, one day, he said to me, 'Oh, give the kid the dam.'" The dam was built. Then Johnson had to persuade the Rural Electrification Administration and other agencies to finance the laying of thousands of miles of wire across large areas where there was nowhere near the minimum residential density— something like seven people per square mile—the REA required. The story of how Lyndon Johnson persuaded them to bring the lights to the Hill Country is a noble example of the use of government to help people do something that they could never do for themselves.

Every step was hard. Many of the ranchers didn't want to sign up for the electricity. These were not well-educated people, and they had to grant easements to the government to put the lines across the land. Easements looked like legal documents, and they knew you never wanted to sign anything that had to do with your land because that was putting debt on the land, and you might lose it. Johnson, the political genius, finally found a way to get the people to sign up. It was the women who got their husbands to sign up because the line he used was, "If you do this, you won't look like your mother." The last of his district did not receive electricity for twelve years, but they got it. And all over the Hill Country, people began to name their children for Lyndon Johnson.

This one man had changed the lives of 200,000 people. He brought them into the twentieth century. I understood what Tommy Corcoran meant when he said, "That kid was the best congressman for a district that ever was."

So we see the seeds of the Great Society in the young Lyndon Johnson. We see in that young congressman's battle to bring the lights not only the compassion he was to display as president but the rare gift that made that compassion meaningful: the gift for mobilizing the powers of government to ease people's needs.

Unfortunately, that's not all we see in the young

Lyndon Johnson. There is a side that is as dark as the other side is bright. He was the best congressman for a district that ever was, but all he wanted, from the moment he got to Congress, was to get out of the district, to run for the Senate. In fact, he started running for the Senate three years after he was elected to the House. He lost then, but as soon as he could, he ran again.

And when he realized after the first race that he wouldn't get to the Senate unless he switched sides, he switched sides completely. Texas was then dominated by the oil, natural gas, and sulfur businesses. Their main interest in government, both state and national, was to make sure that it didn't interfere with them. The payment in taxes of even a low share of the billions of dollars they were taking out of the soil would have enabled the Texas government to improve the lot of the people. But they didn't want to pay any taxes. These were the Texas Regulars, the worst reactionaries. They hated the working man, they hated labor unions, they hated blacks, they hated Jews, and they hated Roosevelt. In return for their support, Lyndon Johnson made himself their willing tool.

Betrayal was one of his methods. When he came to the conclusion that Roosevelt couldn't help him with his greater ambitions, he turned against Roosevelt in an instant. Much sadder was his betrayal of Sam Rayburn, the Speaker of the House. For two decades, Rayburn ruled the House of Representatives as no one had ruled it before or has since. He was a uniquely honest man. He never wrote memos for the record; he never wrote memos to himself. When he walked through the halls of Congress, people were always asking for this favor or that. Someone once asked, "Don't you need to make notes to remember what you promised?" And he said, "If you always tell the truth, you don't need to make notes to remember what you said." An astonishing number of the measures for which we give the credit only to Roosevelt would not have become law if Rayburn hadn't, through the unique force of his personality, rammed them through a very conservative House of Representatives.

Rayburn always wanted a wife and children. But he was married for only a short period. We don't know why the marriage ended, and he never married again. He was uneasy with women, uneasy in social situations. He hated to go to parties.

During the week he was the center of attention. He was the ruler of the House, surrounded by people asking favors. But on weekends, everyone else left. They went back to their families. Rayburn was alone. A proud man, he would walk the streets around the Capitol with his face set grimly, as if he didn't want anyone to bother him, as if he wanted to be alone. But his young assistants knew the truth because sometimes it got to be too much for him. He once said, "Loneliness is what breaks a man. Loneliness is what breaks the heart." Sometimes on a Sunday, he would call the assistants down to the office as if he had something urgent for them to do, and they would watch him sitting behind his desk, pulling open drawers as if he really had some reason to be there.

When Lyndon Johnson first came to Washington, as secretary to a congressman, he had an in with Rayburn because his father had known Rayburn in the Texas legislature. And he and Lady Bird started to invite Sam Rayburn to Sunday breakfast or brunch at their small apartment. Lady Bird would make chili the hot Texas way that Speaker Sam liked. She made peach ice cream. And after breakfast the two men would sit there with the Sunday papers, talking.

Rayburn became almost like a father to Lyndon. Once, while Lady Bird was in Texas on vacation, Lyndon got pneumonia, which in that era was very serious. Rayburn sat next to his hospital bed all night. A chain smoker, Rayburn was afraid that he would wake Johnson if he brushed the ashes off his clothes. When Johnson woke up, there was the Speaker, his vest covered with ashes. And as soon as Rayburn saw that Johnson was awake, he leaned over him and said, "Lyndon, never worry about anything. If you ever need anything, call on me."

Johnson soon did call on him. Roosevelt was creating a

new agency: the National Youth Administration. Each state was going to have its own director, and Johnson wanted the Texas job. When Rayburn proposed this to the White House, he was greeted with laughs. Johnson was twenty-six or twenty-seven. He had no administrative experience. Why would they put him in charge of a whole major New Deal agency?

There is a passage in the memoirs of Texas senator Tom Connolly that deals with this: "Yesterday, an astounding thing happened. Sam Rayburn came to see me. Everybody knows that Sam never asks a man for a favor. But he asked me for a favor yesterday and he would not leave my office until I granted it." That favor, of course, was for Connolly to use his power as chairman of the Foreign Relations Committee to get the NYA appointment for Johnson. Johnson's career was on its way.

But a few years later FDR needed a man in Texas to distribute New Deal patronage and projects. His former man in Texas had been John Garner, his vice president, but Garner and Roosevelt were now on the outs. Rayburn was the logical choice to replace him. But Lyndon Johnson wanted this job for himself. Although no one was more loyal to Roosevelt than Rayburn, Johnson convinced Roosevelt that Rayburn had in effect turned against him—and Johnson became Roosevelt's man in Texas.

I'll never forget learning about this betrayal of Rayburn. I had spent a lot of time interviewing the now elderly men who once had been Sam Rayburn's young assistants and interviewing elderly congressmen. I had learned about Rayburn's loneliness, and I understood how much he needed those Sundays at Johnson's apartment. Then I was sitting in the Lyndon Johnson Library and going through papers. And gradually, as I was reading the intra-office memos and the telephone calls and the telegrams from many different files, I began to see unfolding what had happened between Roosevelt and Rayburn and the role Johnson had played. I went outside and walked around the library because I didn't want to come back up there and find out that it meant what it seemed to. But of course the letters meant exactly what I thought.

The major problem in writing about Lyndon Johnson's early life was his desire for secrecy, his skill at conceal-ment. The nation saw some of this when he was president, but it went all the way back to his earliest days in politics. When he was a high school teacher, he coached the debat-ing team at a high school in Houston. After he went to Washington to be the congressman's secretary, he corre-sponded with two of his young debaters. And on each let-ter, they told me, he wrote, "Burn this." They were just ordinary letters that a teacher would write to a former stu-dent. Even so, "Every time he came back, the first thing he would ask you is, 'Did you burn my letters?'" One of the former debaters showed me a letter on which was in fact written in Lyndon Johnson's handwriting, "Burn this."

He also arranged to have cut out of his college yearbook—out of hundreds of copies of the yearbook—pages that dealt with certain unsavory things that he did. He would go to incredible lengths to conceal the facts of his past.

He was the greatest of storytellers. And he told anecdotes about his boyhood and his early political career that were so vivid and believable that they were told over and over in biographies and in thousands of newspaper and magazine articles. There was an accepted, oft-repeated version of his life. So when I was starting my work on his biography, I never thought I would have to do extensive research on his youth.

As I was interviewing people in the Hill Country, however, I started to get an inkling that basic elements of the story of Lyndon Johnson's youth were substantially different from the ones depicted in books and articles. As I heard about this terrible, poverty-stricken youth; conflict with his father; the humiliations of being from a family that was the laughingstock of this little town, I realized I was hearing something very important, but I couldn't put the whole picture together.

When Lyndon Johnson was in the White House, his brother, Sam Houston Johnson, was a drunkard. But more important for a biographer, he was one of those people who always talk with such bravado that you are wary of trusting him. Finally, after I checked out a number of things that he told me and they weren't true, I decided not to rely on him.

But then, after two or three years, one day I was walking around Johnson City and suddenly there was Sam Houston coming toward me. He stopped to talk, and I immediately saw a difference. It turned out that he had had cancer, a terrible bout. He had stopped drinking and become somewhat religious. But more than that, he was calmer, more quiet. He was just a more serious man. I decided to try him again.

What I really wanted most to know about by this time was the relationship between Lyndon Johnson and his father. I knew that whatever made Lyndon Johnson this complex, larger-than-life personality, it all came out of his home life.

The National Park Service had re-created the Lyndon Johnson boyhood home, and it looked exactly like it did when Lyndon Johnson had been growing up there. I got permission to take Sam Houston in after closing hours, so we'd be the only two people there. I took him into the dining room, where there was a long, plank table. At one end was a chair for the father, at the other end a chair for the mother, and there was a long bench on either side. On one side sat the three sisters and on the other Lyndon and Sam Houston. I sat Sam Houston where he had sat as a boy, and I said, "Now, Sam, I want you to re-create for me these terrible fights that Lyndon used to have with his father."

His memories came back slowly, and there were long pauses. I had to prompt him: "Well, then, what would your father say?" And then: "What would Lyndon say?" But gradually the inhibitions fell away. He was back in his boyhood. He started talking faster and faster. Finally he was acting it out—the father, for example, shouting, "Lyndon, goddammit, you're a failure. You'll be a failure all your life." And I felt he was able to re-create, as faithfully as anyone can, what had happened in their boyhood. And I said, "I want you to go back and tell me all those stories that you told before, the stories that Lyndon Johnson told everybody. Tell them to me again, but give me more details."

And Sam Houston said, "I can't." And I said, "Why not?" There was a long pause, and then he said, "Because they never happened." And without any further prodding he basically related the outline of Lyndon Johnson's youth—which was very different from the story Lyndon had told. And this time, when I would go back to the other people who were involved in each episode, they'd say, "Yes, that's exactly what happened, and I also remember this and that." Everything was confirmed.

Lyndon Johnson tried to write his own legend, and he almost succeeded. If people like his brother and his boyhood companions and his college classmates hadn't been alive when I came along, he would have succeeded. The seeds of everything that came later in the presidency, and that changed America in so many ways for the better and for the worse, are in the young Lyndon Johnson. In my opinion his presidency was so important for America that we have to know him—the dark side as well as the bright. In my opinion America can't fully understand its history without knowing Lyndon Johnson.

CHAPTER FIVE

RICHARD M. NIXON

"I GAVE THEM A SWORD"

BY BENJAMIN C. BRADLEE

★

The late Philip Graham, head of the Washington Post Company, coined the brilliant definition of journalism as "the first rough draft of history." For us first-rough-draft historians, much of history is anecdotal—almost accidentally gathered on the wing. We try endlessly to answer that most interesting of all questions, "What was he like?" From our own firsthand knowledge, we never get the answer exactly right, but ideally, we get closer every time we add a new anecdote to the historical file.

Richard Nixon was a truly interesting man. I never met a political historian who could resist sharing opinions about him. The first time I remember hearing anything about Nixon, other than what I had read in the newspapers, was from Christian Herter, the patrician politician from Boston who was then a member of Congress. He was telling some friends about a delegation of congressmen he had led on a tour of World War II countries, studying European recovery and the workings of the Marshall Plan. My father asked him, "What was Nixon like?" and I remember Herter pausing for a long time. He had sort of a crooked smile, and he said, "I never saw anyone work harder, but he didn't seem to be having any fun at all." I think that's quite important, because he didn't seem to be having any fun at all at any of the times I saw him.

I spent the next seven years in Europe, where Nixon appeared on my screen primarily as a collateral figure in the embarrassment surrounding Roy Cohn and David Schine, the strange communist-hunters sent by Senator Joseph McCarthy to purge U.S. Information Agency libraries in Europe of books by suspicious "communist sympathizers" like Theodore White, the author who went on to glory as the creator of a series of books titled *The Making of the President.*

When I came back from Europe to work in the Washington bureau of *Newsweek,* Richard Nixon was suddenly much more front and center: My first big story, in fact, was the presidential campaign of 1960.

At first I was covering Jack Kennedy, not Nixon, and that seemed like the best of all worlds. Kennedy was an attractive, easy-to-like man who enjoyed the company of newspapermen. Nixon, by stark contrast, seemed uncomfortable, not easy to like. Even President Eisenhower never seemed all that friendly toward his vice president. Once, at a press conference, Eisenhower was asked to give one example of a major idea proposed by Nixon and then adopted by the Eisenhower administration. He looked puzzled for a while and finally snapped, "If you give me a week, I might think of one."

Benjamin C. Bradlee

A month before the election, *Newsweek*'s editors asked me to swap places with the correspondent who was covering Nixon. I joined the Nixon campaign in Long Island, and here is an excerpt from what I wrote:

> Standing on the back of a truck outside a Long Island arena one night last week, Richard Nixon kept his promise to a crowd of 2,500 people who had not been able to squeeze in to hear his main speech. "I told you I'd bring Pat out to see you, and here she is!" the vice president said, introducing his wife. "Now I ask you, isn't she wonderful? Wasn't she worth waiting for?"

I was comparing the two campaigns, and I wrote: "For Nixon, introducing Pat to the crowd was easy and natural, for he regards her as an essential member of his political team. Jack Kennedy would no more parade his wife on a political platform than he would paint the White House green." In fact, it took Kennedy three weeks of campaigning just to bring himself to explain his wife's absence, by saying, "My wife's home having another baby."

That was just one sample of the enormous differences between the two. In campaigning, Kennedy did not shun a bookish image. Nixon kept it folksy. In Cleveland, for instance, before a sweating, shirt-sleeve crowd of 100,000 people, Senator Kennedy cited six historical or literary quotations in fifteen minutes, including one from an eighteenth-century Speaker of the Connecticut House of Representatives. Nixon would no more adorn his speeches like that than he would pull down the columns of the Capitol. In six days of campaigning through Arkansas, Tennessee, West Virginia, and New England, he never quoted anyone more esoteric than a little girl in Omaha or a little old woman in Moscow or Warsaw.

During the campaign I was selected as one of the pool reporters to cover the first televised debate. We had no idea how powerful a force television was going to be in presidential politics. It's hard now to remember how new it was then. It's hard to remember, too, how naturally JFK mastered the medium and how unflattering TV was to Richard Nixon.

Not only was this my first presidential campaign, but I had become a friend and neighbor of Kennedy, and the rest of the press knew that. The big powers of the press establishment watched the debates on TV sets in a room off the studio. But I was their guy inside, watching the candidates get made up. I had to be careful that I did not tilt my coverage toward anybody.

From inside the studio, I thought Kennedy waxed Nixon. He was cooler. He appeared to be more relaxed. He sweated much less. I felt sorry for Nixon. He was not only sweating noticeably, despite the freezing air-conditioning, but he had been very sick from a leg infection, and he looked it. When I got back to give my report, the old-timers were saying that they thought the debate was a tie. One even suggested that those who heard the debate on the radio would rate it as a Nixon win.

Nixon pretty much disappeared from the Washington scene after that election, and I didn't run into him again until the 1962 gubernatorial election in California, when *Newsweek* asked me to write a cover story on the race between the former vice president and Governor Pat Brown.

For me, it was kind of a reprise of the Kennedy-Nixon campaign. Again, the differences between the two candidates were so striking. It took only minutes to arrange what turned out to be three hours with Pat Brown. I spent a morning with him on the campaign trail. He and his chauffeur sat in the front seat of the state limo, and I was alone in the back. The interview started quickly. Governor Brown wheeled around and said, "How come all you guys from the East always describe me as some kind of a bumbling horse's ass?" That kicked off a truly interesting discussion of Beltway insularity. The whole interview was far removed from the usual banalities of state politics. "I'd beat Nixon by 500,000 votes if the election were held today," said Brown. Politicians never make a prediction like that a short time before an election.

By contrast, it took days for the supercooperative Herb Klein, Nixon's press secretary, to get me any time with the former vice president. And when he finally did, I had to settle for just twenty minutes. Most of that Nixon devoted to a sort of minifilibuster: "There's nothing I resent more than the vicious charges that I will cut aid to the aged, blind, and handicapped." Now, most people don't talk that way. But Richard Nixon did: "I'm going to cut taxes so people up and down the state can spend it at home."

Nixon drew bigger crowds than Brown. "It's the celebrity thing," the former vice president explained, almost condescendingly. But Pat Brown did, in the end, beat him—by almost 300,000 votes. And a few weeks later the real Richard Nixon was talking to us reporters from his baffled heart: "You won't have Nixon to kick around anymore, because, gentlemen, this is my last press conference."

The next time I encountered him was eight years later. By then we were both in new jobs: I as executive editor of the *Washington Post* and Richard Nixon as president of the United States.

The *Post* was an extremely informal place on Saturday mornings. We worked six days a week, often seven. And the wives had begun to insist that since we were going to work on that schedule, perhaps we would take the children to work with us on Saturdays so the wives could sleep in. The children spent the morning answering the phones and Xeroxing their hands.

One Saturday morning someone's child answered my telephone and tracked me down in the city room to say the White House was on the line. I knew the child and I liked him, but I thought it was probably humor columnist Art Buchwald calling about having lunch and trying a joke. But damned if it wasn't the White House. "Mr. Bradlee, would you hold, sir, for the president?" said the operator. And then he was on the line.

I had no idea why he was calling. I glanced quickly at the front page of the paper but saw nothing that might have made him angry. We began exchanging pleasantries.

"Glad to see you're working Saturdays, Ben," said the president. And then he started talking about the war—our war, Nixon's and mine, "the Big Two," as my children call it. He started talking about when he was a young naval officer in Washington. I thought I remembered that he had worked for the Office of Price Administration as a navy officer, fixing the price of tires. We talked tires. Then he was telling me that we ought to talk like this more often, and he said good-bye.

The next Saturday he called again. This time I was ready with a list of questions. But he was simply trying to schmooze. No interviews. This lasted another ten minutes, and that was it. We never talked again. Somebody obviously had told him that he should try to chat up the editor of the *Post*. But he wasn't very good at it, and he knew it. He made a valiant effort, then gave up.

That was two years before Watergate. It was also only months before the Pentagon Papers battle, when the Nixon administration took the *New York Times* and the *Washington Post* all the way to the Supreme Court to prevent us from publishing this study of how the United States had got bogged down in the Vietnam War.

The *New York Times* had the Pentagon Papers first. And one Sunday morning they published miles and miles of copy. The agony of being beaten really badly was substantial. For the next three days, the *Post* tried to play catch-up ball, and finally we got hold of the papers. We printed the first installment the next morning. While we were trying to read 4,000 pages and make sense of them, we were also fighting with the lawyers, who were telling us we couldn't write anything because after running a couple of installments, the *New York Times* had been enjoined by a federal judge from publishing. It was the first time in the history of the republic that a newspaper had been enjoined with the doctrine of prior restraint.

We finally decided that we would print. Katharine Graham, who was our leader, gave the okay. There was round-the-clock litigation. And on the second day, we, too, were enjoined.

★

Benjamin C. Bradlee

I still don't quite understand Richard Nixon's reaction to the Pentagon Papers. The government had never before tried to stop a paper from publishing. What's more, the Pentagon Papers themselves dealt with events that ended in 1967, almost two years before Nixon became president. I think the lesson was that he was going to get the *New York Times* and the *Washington Post* one way or another.

In the course of the battle, we went up and we went down. We lost. We appealed. We won on appeal. They appealed. We lost. Then it started all the way up the ladder again. And finally, in ten days, we got to the Supreme Court, where we "won," six to three, which is not an overwhelming win—especially when the three were all saying, "Don't go after them civilly; go after them criminally."

The civil statute was repeated in the criminal statute, and it says, "Whoever knowingly publishes information that they believe will damage the national security of the United States is guilty of treason."

Treason!

Eighteen years later, the government's chief prosecutor in that case, Solicitor General Erwin Griswold, former dean of the Harvard Law School, stated flatly that there was never a matter of national security involved.

What kind of man pursues that kind of behavior? It seemed to me then, and I have since seen little reason to change my mind, that we were beginning to see the results of an inferiority complex—some internal feelings against the press, against the East, against the Ivy League.

And that was only one dark corner of this complicated man. Nixon never seemed comfortable in his own skin. Even a walk on the beach in his beloved San Clemente would more likely be taken in wingtips than bare feet. That stiffness perhaps helps to explain why he seemed more at ease exercising presidential power in foreign affairs than when he had to engage in the parochial politics of an unruly Congress or deal with the governors of key electoral states. Or, God forbid, the press.

His breakthrough with China showed him at his presidential best. It also displayed his acute understanding of his personal power over the political right. His bona fides with the conservative wing of his party gave him the power to take the China initiative—and he used it.

When he was detached, Nixon could see with great subtlety the implication of actions. The story about Chicago mayor Richard Daley delivering enough graveyard votes for Kennedy to win one of the narrowest victories in the history of presidential politics is well known. Some say that Nixon made a very statesmanlike, unselfish decision in not protesting voting irregularities. He felt, they suggest, that it could weaken the country to have no one clearly in charge while the dispute went on. But as someone who covered the story closely—I was the reporter who quoted Daley's remark to JFK on election night: "With a little luck and the help of a few close friends, we're gonna win. We're gonna take Illinois"—I am not so sure of Nixon's altruism.

What actually happened was this: Nixon sent William P. Rogers, who would later become his attorney general, to check on the situation. Rogers reported back that however many votes were cast illegally by Democrats in Chicago and Cook County, just as many were probably cast illegally by Republicans in downstate Illinois. I am almost certain that Nixon would have found it irresistible to protest the illegal votes had it not been for the fact that his own party might have been doing the same thing. He made a political decision: The risk was too great. He certainly had the power to protest, but for not entirely statesmanlike reasons chose not to use it.

One way to analyze presidential power is to look at how effectively it is used to attract people of real distinction into an administration. Franklin Roosevelt, John Kennedy, and Lyndon Johnson, for instance, attracted exceptional people to serve with them. But on this score I think Nixon rates very low—with two exceptions. One was Henry Kissinger, who, when he was not campaigning for the Nobel Peace Prize, displayed a powerful intellect. Another was Secretary of Commerce Pete Peterson, a person of quality and high integrity.

One reason for the lack of heavyweights in Nixon's administration was that he was a tough sell to the East Coast intellectuals, who never forgave his attacks on Helen Gahagan Douglas in the 1950 campaign for the U.S. Senate. Like LBJ, who was a graduate of Southwest Texas State, Nixon, a graduate of Whittier, felt somewhat inferior to Ivy League types and was ever suspicious of the biases of the *New York Times,* the *Washington Post,* and the television networks. As a result, and not surprisingly, the inner circle he created had a California cast. Its members shared Nixon's suspicions and dislikes and went on the offense when they came to power. It is also important to remember that Nixon had served for eight years under Eisenhower, whose closest advisers came predictably from the Republican business establishment—from what Adlai Stevenson called "the green fairways of indifference." They were capable but not particularly visionary.

I get so angry when I hear some people ask, "What the hell's the difference between Watergate and Whitewater?" Watergate was a scandalous political melodrama that ended up with the resignation of a disgraced president and the jailing of more than forty people, including the attorney general of the United States, the White House chief of staff, the White House counsel, and the president's chief domestic adviser. By comparison, the Whitewater case petered out to become something a little seedy: a little bit of hanky-panky on some cattle futures, maybe; some guy trying to make a buck or two on a land deal. It hardly seemed to threaten the pillars of the Constitution.

The Watergate tapes gave an insight into Nixon and the more unworthy ways he used his power that people may have lost sight of. People forget how much was on tape—3,700 hours. Less than forty hours were released, and that was enough to bring him down.

Nixon struggled ferociously to gain control of the tapes and keep them locked away. He struggled so intensely, with such determination, because of his fear that the contents of the tapes would cripple his hopes for a historical resurrection and rehabilitation, in the words of historian Stanley Kutler.

At first Nixon tried to get away with releasing a censored version. All references to Jesus Christ were removed. All "goddamns" were changed to "damn." And the tapes were scrubbed clean of the dreaded *f* word, which in fact was used often in the conversations.

It was April of 1996, twenty-two years after Congress passed a law releasing the Nixon tapes at the earliest reasonable date, nineteen years after the Supreme Court validated that law, nine years after the National Archives finished processing the tapes for public release, five years after litigation and mediation and two years after Nixon's death, before the tapes were finally in the public domain.

The specific line and the cover-up are pretty well known. What we may have forgotten is what Kutner calls "the crudities of thought and language" revealed on the tapes: the vulgarities, the stunning prejudices, the jagged cynicism of this man.

Nixon repeatedly speaks—pejoratively and insultingly —about Jews. "Bob," he says to Haldeman in September 1971, "please get me the names of the Jews. You know, the big Jewish contributors of the Democrats. Could you please investigate some of the _____?" And here he uses a term never printed in a family newspaper. "What about the rich Jews? The IRS is full of Jews, so go after them like a son of a bitch."

He later suggests reviving the House Un-American Activities Committee: "What a marvelous opportunity for the committee. They'll be hanging from the rafters, going after all those Jews. Just find one that is a Jew, will you?" In defending his use of the "plumbers," the group operating illegally—ostensibly, to plug leaks—Nixon says, "This is national security. We've got all sorts of activities because we've been trying to run this town by avoiding the Jews in the government."

What if your friendly newspaper editor talked like that? He would be pumping gas, I can promise you. What if your friendly college president talked like that? It's really unthinkable. There is a remarkable contrast between this Nixon and the image Nixon created of himself as upstanding, moral, churchgoing man; devoted father; dog lover; and on and on.

He is wondrous to read. One of my all-time favorite quotes from the Nixon tapes came after he had authorized the break-in of the office of Daniel Ellsberg's psychiatrist. Think of the president of the United States occupying himself with that. As he concludes the discussion, he catches himself: "I believe somehow I have to avoid having the president approve the break-in of a psychiatrist's office." He was looking for that place in history all the time.

Finally, of course, these are the tapes that convicted Richard Nixon in the court of public opinion. In 1977 he told an interviewer, "I brought myself down. I gave them a sword and they stuck it in. And I guess if I'd been in their position, I'd have done the same thing."

A self-destructive man, then. And in the quiet of time, he admitted it.

CHAPTER SIX

RONALD REAGAN

FORCE OF NATURE

★

BY EDMUND MORRIS

★

After Ronald Reagan was nominated as the Republican candidate for president of the United States in the summer of 1980, he set up his headquarters at a farm in the Middleburg district of Virginia, not far from Washington, D.C. He was then sixty-nine years old. And if, as seemed increasingly likely, he was going to be elected president, he would be taking the oath in January 1981, just a few weeks short of his seventieth birthday.

The estate that would be his home for the next couple of months was owned by a Texas zillionaire (Governor William Clements) who had kindly made it available to him. On the very first morning of Reagan's stay, the sound of chopping was heard out front. His entourage snuck their curtains back and looked out, and there was Ronald Reagan in the dawn's early light, chopping down a tree in front of the house. A tree that precisely and beautifully dissected the vista of lawn, fields, forests, and the distant blue ridge of the Virginia mountains. Reagan was quietly chopping it down. After it had fallen, he was asked why he had axed it. And he said with that beguiling simplicity of his, "Because it spoils the view."

Now as a biographer—which is to say, a student of

human behavior—I'm fascinated by this story. It raises some fundamental questions about the kind of man who seeks the presidency of the United States. Had Reagan been an ordinary person, one would simply say, "How could he *do* that? It wasn't his house; it wasn't his view; it wasn't his tree." But Ronald Reagan was not an ordinary man. He was indeed extraordinary. So the questions are more complex. Why was it so urgently necessary for him to rearrange the landscape? Why was it done without consultation? Why didn't anybody rush out and stop him? Why did they wait until after the fact before they asked him for an explanation? Why, in short, did Ronald Reagan get exactly what he wanted that morning, as he always had, from the time he was a teenage boy?

The answer is both simple and mysterious, and it applies to all natural leaders—male or female, Western or Eastern, sophisticated or savage. He chopped down that tree—and by the way, I can't help wondering if the young George Washington had the same lack of scruples when he chopped down his—because it was his nature to eliminate obstacles. It was not his nature to consider the feelings of the tree's owner or, for that matter, the feelings of the tree. His heart told him the tree had to go. His brain told him that the landscape would be better off without it. The question of contrary feelings of opposition and criticism simply didn't arise. Taking the immortal words of

Lewis Carroll, he was judge; he was jury; he was cunning old Fury.

The odd thing about Ronald Reagan was that although you might think that particular act crude and rude, even barbaric, he was in person both kindly and gentlemanly. He was *gentle* and gentlemanly. Never was there anyone with less personal hostility or desire to hurt. He had a curious dislike of confrontation. He tended to shy away from any private expressions of emotion that conflicted with his own. He was too polite to disagree with people face to face. He used jokes and humor to deflect intimacy, to deflect displays of emotion, which he considered unseemly. He did not like people who "slopped over" in his presence.

Mike Deaver, his aide, tells a story of Romauld Spasowski, the Polish ambassador to the United States, who defected in December 1981 and came to the White House. At that time he was the most senior defector from an eastern bloc country in our history. An old Polish aristocrat. He came to explain to President Reagan what it was like to have to give up his country, to betray the feelings and convictions of a lifetime, to separate himself from his native land and from his family. He and his wife were sitting side by side on the couch in the Oval Office, weeping. Deaver confesses that he was weeping, too. It was an agonizing moment, and Reagan sat there—twinkling.

The strange thing is that in nonprivate situations he

was all compassion. If he had stepped into the Rose Garden, where the press was waiting, and told the same story the ambassador had just told him, I can guarantee his voice would have shaken, his eyes would have glittered, and he would have exuded real emotion—because that was his nature: He was a public person. He was theatrical in the best sense of the word. His emotions were lived out and expressed in public.

In private, as I discovered to my consternation when I started interviewing him, he was almost distressingly cool. It was very hard to get a reaction out of him. In the last weeks of 1988, toward the end of his presidency, he let me spend two complete days with him. I dogged his footsteps from the moment he stepped out of the elevator in the morning till the moment he went back upstairs. Within hours I was a basket case, simply because I discovered that to be a president, even just to stand behind him and watch him deal with everything that comes toward him, is to be constantly besieged by supplications, emotional challenges, problems, catastrophes, whines.

For example, that first morning I'm waiting outside the elevator in the White House with his personal aide, Jim Kuhn. The doors open, out comes Ronald Reagan giving off waves of cologne, looking as usual like a million bucks, and Jim says to him, "Well, Mr. President, your first appointment this morning is going to be a Louisiana state trooper. You're going to be meeting him as we go through the Conservatory en route to the Oval Office. This guy had his eyes shot out in the course of duty a year ago. He's here to receive an award from you and get photographed, and he's brought his wife and his daughter. You'll have to spend a few minutes with him, just a grip-and-grin, and then we're going on to your senior staff meeting."

So around the corner we go, and I'm following behind Reagan's well-tailored back, and there is this state trooper, eyes shot out, aware of the fact that the president is coming —he could hear our footsteps. And there's his wife, coruscating with happiness. It's the biggest moment of their lives. There, too, is their little girl. Reagan walks up, introduces himself to the trooper, gives him the double handshake—the hand over the hand, the magic touch of flesh —and expertly turns him so the guy understands they are going to be photographed. The photograph is taken, a nice word or two is exchanged with his wife. It lasted about thirty-five seconds. On to the Oval Office.

By the way, Reagan said to me as we walked along, "You know the biblical saying about an eye for an eye and a tooth for a tooth? I sure would like to get both eyes of the bastard that shot that policeman." In other words, he was as moved as I was. But he had magnificently concealed it.

A president has to deal with this kind of thing all day, every day, for four or eight years. He therefore has to be the kind of person who is expert at controlling emotion, at not showing too much of it—containing himself; otherwise, he is going to be sucked dry in no time at all and lose his ability to function in public.

Gerry Rafshoon, who managed President Carter's campaign advertising in 1976, told me about going the rounds with Carter, who was an old friend. "Jimmy and I were buddies," he said. "We slept in the same hotel rooms. We were in each other's company all the time. We were just two guys on the road. But," Rafshoon said, "the moment he was elected, this glass wall came down, and it was never the same since. I felt this cool, transparent barrier between me and the president. So I perfectly understand the way you are with Reagan. They all have to be like that—self-protective."

When Reagan was confronted with difficult situations, if he was not able to deflect them with his jokes—and he almost invariably *was* able, because he had a delicious and superabundant sense of humor—he would sometimes retreat into silence. He modeled himself on Calvin Coolidge, I think, in that sense. (He liked the "cool" in Coolidge.) Coolidge was famous for never saying a word when people came to see him, because as he explained, "It just encourages them."

Reagan, being a naturally garrulous man, needed some restraint to keep himself quiet. I was interested to come across this just the other day—too late, as a matter of fact, to put in the text of my book. (It's there as a footnote.) Reagan's White House counsel, a man named Peter Wallison, very kindly let me read his diary of his years in the White House, 1986 and 1987. It seems that Wallison had to deal with the phenomenon of a bearded, independent biographer stalking around the building (I came on board, by the way, in November of 1985). Some arrangement had to be arrived at to take care of the fact that I was not a staff member, polluting with my literary presence the very nature of executive privilege. Wallison, as the president's counsel, had to figure out a way in which my presence would be tolerable and not infringe on the security of the United States. And he also had to take care of Reagan's personal interests, one of which was that when the president left office he was going to be writing his own autobiography.

So I'm reading Wallison's diary years later, and I find this entry for September 17, 1986: "I met with the Pres. about Edmund Morris. He expressed some impatience, saying that he was already three minutes late for his next appointment. [Reagan was a meticulous timekeeper.] I told the president there was a potential conflict of interest between Edmund Morris's biography and the president's own memoirs, and that he might consider not answering some of the questions that Morris might pose, particularly questions about the state of his mind when he arrived at decisions. I said that this was material that should go into his own memoirs, and that if it is given to Morris, the memoirs may have less value and may in fact be contradicted by what Morris has been told. I mentioned that I had also talked with Mrs. R about this, and Nancy had agreed."

Here's the interesting part: "During all this time, the Pres. was staring at me very directly, not saying anything, and with no expression on his face. Perhaps it was the light, but the pupils of his eyes seemed to be bright points—somewhat disconcerting. The president eventually said he had selected Morris because he was impressed with Morris's book on T. Roosevelt, and he would keep all this in mind. But I do not think that he was persuaded."

What intrigues me about this diary entry is the *silence*, the enigmatic silence with which Reagan received this conscientious advice from his lawyer. Reagan was a very fair man. He understood what Wallison was saying, but nevertheless he also understood that he had given me a privilege—to come to the White House and write a book about him—and it was not in his nature to be unfair and withhold himself from me. Because he *was* fair, he *was* honorable. He was presidential. He had none of the killer instinct that I observed in President Carter, for example.

Shortly after Carter left the White House, I met with him at Princeton University with a bunch of other presidential scholars. Carter wanted some free advice on how to write his *me-moirs,* as he pronounced them. (A significant mispronunciation. "How do you-all think Ah should begin my *me-moirs?*") When my turn came I said, "Well, Mr. President, I think you should begin with that great moment after you were inaugurated, and you got out of the presidential limo, and you and Rosalynn walked along Pennsylvania Avenue hand in hand in the sunshine." I said, "After the claustrophobia of the Nixon and Ford years, to see the president of the United States walking in the open air like that was a marvelous moment." I did not add that it was all downhill from there. And I said, "Maybe you can describe that, and then flash back to the point from which you came."

Carter said, "No, no, Ah'm gonna start with the moment Ah triumphed over Scoop Jackson in the Florida primary." So we're all thinking, "The Florida primary? What's he talking about? He used the word 'triumphed'?" He was thinking about a primary where for the first time he achieved the intoxicating realization that he might be winning this race for the nomination and the presidency. That was a supreme moment for Carter. And when he said, "Ah *triumphed* over Scoop Jackson," his eyes flashed such blue flame that I was reminded of my juvenile science fiction comics, with blue flames shooting out of ray guns. I thought to myself, "This guy is a killer." Reagan never flashed blue fire. His ambition and his force were at once more formidable and more benign.

Theodore Roosevelt was also a man of overwhelming force—a cutter-down of trees in the metaphorical sense. He was famously aggressive. There was nothing he loved more than to decimate wildlife. I first became aware of him as a small boy in Kenya, when the city of Nairobi, where I was born, published its civic history. The book contained a photograph of this American president with a pith helmet and mustache and clicking teeth and spectacles. He had come to Kenya from the White House in 1910 and proceeded to shoot every living thing in the landscape. I remember as a ten-year-old boy looking at this picture of this man and, as small boys do, saying to myself, "He looks as though he is fun. I'd like to spend time with that guy." I was conscious even as a child not only of the sweetness of his personality but of this feeling of *force* that a smudgy old photograph could not obscure.

It is fascinating to study the speech-patterns of presidential oratory. Theodore Roosevelt, for instance, had an affection for the letter *p*. He loved plosives, words like "power." He would have popped every microphone in the United States if he had been living in the technological age. His voice was not beautiful like Reagan's. It was a harsh, high-pitched voice, and those teeth of his used to cut off syllables—snap, snap—as though he were biting out the word. And his *p*s would pop with Gatling-gun force. The effect of his oratory was to bury every word in the psyche of his listeners. He fired off his words in his speeches with this physical, motive violence that gave listeners the feeling that behind was a mental force that could not be resisted.

Now, Reagan's voice, which was a large part of Reagan's power, was indeed beautiful. Even in his teenage years it was unusual, a light, very fluid baritone, quick and silvery. It had a fuzzy husk to it, rather like peach fuzz. And there was something sensually appealing about it—so much so that people got physical pleasure out of listening to Reagan talk. He was a very fast talker when he was young. As a freshman at Eureka College in the fall of 1928, he was selected by the senior class to proclaim a student strike against the faculty. The president of the college had fired a few faculty in an economy measure, and the students elected to go on strike until the president either resigned or gave them back their beloved professors.

Why did they choose this untested freshman, Ronald Reagan—or "Dutch" Reagan, as he was known in those days—to articulate the motion for them at a midnight meeting in the chapel? Somehow, even at the age of seventeen, Reagan was obviously born to articulate, to speak, to incite, to present. He himself didn't yet realize this. He had indulged in high school theatricals. He loved acting;

he knew he was an actor by nature. What he did not know until the moment he stepped out onto that little platform was that he was a platform personality. He describes it in his memoirs: "Stepping out there, I presented the motion and the crowd came to its feet with a roar. It was heady wine." At that moment, Ronald Reagan was transformed into a politician. He had discovered the delight of shouting at people.

And his voice from that moment on became the expression of his personal drive. Reagan's drive, as I've indicated, was not a brutal force. He smilingly, humorously, beguilingly prevailed throughout life; always seemed to come out on top; always seemed to get exactly what he wanted, in career after career.

He had a narrative life, a sequential one, much more so than most presidents. His first career was that of a radio sportscaster in the early 1930s. His voice took him to that job: even at college. He used to practice with a broomstick, talking to it as though it were a microphone. He would narrate imaginary football games into the broomstick, while the guys at the dorm sat around listening to him. And when he came down from college, the broomstick miraculously mutated into a real microphone in Davenport, Iowa, and he narrated his way into a studio job.

Dutch Reagan was an extremely successful sportscaster. His mellifluous voice beamed out over Iowa and Illinois and the central states, first from WOC–Davenport and then from WHO–Des Moines. It beamed to such a beguiling extent that Hugh Sidey, the presidential correspondent of *Life* magazine, once told me, "You know, I was a Dust Bowl brat in the early 1930s, living in Iowa. I used to hear Dutch Reagan's voice coming through our loudspeaker, and I don't remember anything he said, but that voice persuaded me that although life was terrible at the moment, somehow things were going to get better." He said, "I cannot describe the quality of the voice; it just filled me with optimism." And we saw this come to pass when Reagan eventually became president and filled us almost overnight with a sense of well-being and purposefulness.

I'm sure I don't need to remind many of you what things were like in the late 1970s—the era of American angst. We were an unhappy country. When President Carter wasn't telling us about his hemorrhoids, he was telling us about our national malaise. "Patriotism" was an embarrassing word. Young people were snickering at men and women in uniform. The legacy of Vietnam infected our national discourse. But then something happened at Ronald Reagan's inaugural ceremony in January of 1981—when he stepped in front of the microphone, and with entire predictability the sun burst out and bathed him in a glow. His speech was actually banal. The language did not sing; the sentiments he expressed were clichéd. But there was something about that voice and that physical presence that indefinably and inexplicably made us feel that America was finding its way back to self-respect. The national mood changed overnight.

Let me at this point summarize the narrative sequence of Reagan's life. And let me preface it by a remark his son, a very acute young man, made to me. Ron said, "You know, my father has had all these lives. He was a sportscaster, then he was a film star, then an army officer, then a trade union leader, then a corporate spokesman for General Electric in the 1950s, then he was governor, then he was president, and none of these lives seem to have rubbed off on him."

I must say that it disconcerted me, too, when I first started interviewing the president in late 1985. His ordinariness in the Oval Office, when just the two of us were alone there together, was most surprising. I would have expected him to be as pertinent and masterful and luminous as he was in public, but I found myself talking to a quiet, nondescript, almost dull personality with no particular interest in himself. It was hard for a biographer to handle. There was a complete lack of ego. And I understood what Ron meant. It perplexed me for at least a year until I was sitting with Reagan on the patio of his beloved Rancho del Cielo, "Ranch in the Sky," in southern California.

He had given me a tour of this surpassingly ordinary little house, a cabin that he'd put together practically with his own hands. It had phony tile flooring, an ugly ceiling, horse pictures hanging crooked, a Louis L'Amour novel by his bedside. He takes me out onto the patio and we sit down at a leather table pocked with food stains, beneath a flypaper with dead flies on it, looking out over the valley, and he says, "Isn't it beautiful?" and I said, "Yes, Mr. President, it is very nice." But you know, it was not naturally beautiful. It was a long, manicured—that's the only word I can think of—*manicured* valley, open in the central part, but rising on both sides to a ridge that overlooked the Pacific. And all the madrona trees and live oaks that encircled this valley had been manicured to such an extent— I'm not talking topiary now, I'm just talking about trimming limbs and taking off dead leaves and undergrowth— had been pruned to such an extent that it was not quite real. It looked like a Grant Wood landscape. It was too clean. His idea of beauty was to control the landscape. He had personally, over the past several years, spent all his summers with a hacksaw and the choppers and axes manicuring this landscape to his satisfaction. And then I realized that the ordinariness beside me was indeed extraordinary. It was Reagan's nature to control everything he saw, in his quiet, purposeful way.

I was reminded of Napoleon in exile in Elba after

being defeated in 1812. Even on that flyblown Italian island, the emperor could not stop being the emperor. He
built bridges; he laid roads; he organized village councils.
He ruled; he controlled; he was imperial still, because that
was his nature.

Reagan's way of looking at the world had its funnier
side. I was sitting there on the patio with him and I said,
"Wow, Mr. President, look there. Look at that smog coming up from Santa Barbara." Over the rim of the valley this
brownish haze was moving up into the sky. He said, "That's
not smog." I said, "It's from the Pacific Coast Highway." He
said, "No, that's ozone." I could have produced an envi-
ronmental impact study, I could have shown him the pho-
tometrics, I could have shown him hard evidence, and he
would have still said, "No, that's ozone."

What Reagan believed, he believed with passion. He
photographed it in his mind with such clarity that nothing
could change it afterwards. That kind of mind is in many
ways off-putting. It's a mind that seems unreceptive to cor-
rection. There were times, indeed, when he was confronted with the truth and reacted with sheer anger.
Michael Deaver told me that once in 1973, when Reagan
was still governor, they were talking to him across a table
about the enforced resignation of Vice President Spiro
Agnew, who had had to step down for taking bribes and
corruption in office. Reagan was saying, "You know, it's

really tough what they did to Agnew. I always liked that guy. It was very unfair what happened to him." And Deaver said, "Governor, he took money in office. The guy was a sleazebag. He had to be thrown out." Reagan was playing with a heavy bunch of keys when Deaver said this. He hauled back and threw the keys smack into Deaver's chest—*koodoomp!* He was angry at being confronted with evidence that conflicted with his sentiments.

Now in a way, this is comic and in another way it's scary. But in a situation where the president of the United States is negotiating the future of the world with the general secretary of a monolithic communist power, that's the kind of guy you want to have on your side of the table-tennis net.

Many of you may remember watching on television when Reagan first met Mikhail Gorbachev, in November of 1985. It was a freezing day in Geneva; I was there standing at the curve of the steps, dying of cold. Even the Russian security guards, who one would think would be used to cold, were turning blue around the edges, like ornamental cabbages. Out through the door, as Gorbachev's limousine swept up the driveway, came Ronald Reagan with no overcoat on, looking absolutely magnificent. He came down the steps, met this rather awkward Soviet leader trying to divest himself of scarf and overcoat, and Gorbachev, against all expectations, was the one who was discomfited. Years later, I asked Gorbachev, "At that moment when you met President Reagan for the first time, what did you see when you looked into his eyes? What kind of man did you think you were meeting?" Gorbachev spoke in Russian. And his interpreter said, "Mr. Gorbachev says that Reagan was 'authentic.'" In Russian, the word is *lichnost*. He went on to explain that *lichnost* is not an adjective but an almost untranslatable noun. It means much more than "an authentic human being." It means a man of such force and certainty that he is true right through to his fingertips. He represents not only himself but everything he believes in. And in the case of President Reagan, he represented the force, the personality, the character of the United States.

There was a climactic moment at the Geneva summit during the second afternoon—when, by the way, Gorby and Reagan had come to like each other to such an extent that they couldn't keep their hands off each other. They kept grasping and feeling each other and exchanging fond glances. It was almost sexual—it was a coming together of opposite forces. Anyway, there was this moment where Reagan was being so obstinate on the subject of the Strategic Defense Initiative that Gorbachev, after a silence that Secretary George Shultz said seemed to last for an hour—it was probably only about fifteen seconds or so—Gorbachev threw down his Soviet-made pencil and said, "Mr. President, I can see that I cannot shake your conviction. You believe what you believe."

What he saw in Reagan's eyes was the metaphorical reality of the Strategic Defense Initiative. Scientifically, the SDI was almost unrealizable. But there, floating in Reagan's fertile imagination, were rays neutralizing incoming Soviet missiles, reducing them to radioactive chaff that blew away on the wind of time; a huge, heaven-filling, benign vision that was so potent—I've seen those rays in his eyes myself—that Gorbachev couldn't do anything about it except throw down his pencil. And as we all know, the Strategic Defense Initiative was what brought about the final capitulation of the Soviet Union, starting with its call for total nuclear disarmament at Reykjavik.

That particular summit was depressing to most thinking Westerners because it seemed that Reagan had traded away a golden opportunity for the world to start reducing down to a near-zero nuclear capability on both sides. But because he was so fanatically insistent on continuing with the SDI program, both leaders had to stand up from the table and admit that their second summit had failed.

Reagan came back to the United States deeply disappointed. There was massive spin control at the White House. The summit was presented as a triumph, but from the Western point of view it was bad news—or seemed bad news at that time.

Gorbachev, however, told the prime minister of Iceland, when they were standing under an umbrella together at the airport, "This is not a bad summit. This is not a failure. It is the beginning of the end of the cold war. For the first time, the leaders of the Soviet bloc and the Western bloc have discussed in a realistic fashion the prospect of a world without nuclear arms."

From that moment on, history was more or less determined. It was determined by (this is going to sound like Rudyard Kipling) two strong men from both sides of the earth, who realized that the international balance of terror, after forty years of cold war, had got to the point of insanity: that something had to be done to bring the world back to normality. And these two great men did, in fact, bring about the end of the cold war.

Let me close with an anecdote I find especially poignant. When Reagan confirmed, in his own handwriting, in November of 1994, that he was beginning to suffer from Alzheimer's disease, he uncomplainingly and eloquently accepted the inevitable. I went to see him a few weeks after that and realized that I didn't want to see him again, simply because it was so distressing to see this superabundant, magnificent personality, this beautiful body, this functioning mechanism, beginning to be fallible. I realized that if I continued to hang around, protectiveness would begin to distort the biography I was writing.

One remark he made to me struck me with particular force. He pointed at the shelf in his office where he had a set of volumes, *The Presidential Papers of Ronald Reagan,* and he said, "Those are my . . . trees." He was trying to find the word for "books," but the word that came into his head was "trees." The feller of trees was reduced to thinking that was all his life's achievement had been—a row of regular trunks, a shaped, solid mass. Perhaps so. But history may decide that Reagan's legacy was spiritual as well as substantial.

CHAPTER SEVEN

WILLIAM J. CLINTON

LOSS, RECOVERY, AND JUJITSU

★

BY DAVID MARANISS

★

I think it is safe to say that no previous president of the United States wanted to be president more, and from an earlier age, than Bill Clinton. When he was in the second grade, his mother started going around the neighborhood in Hot Springs, Arkansas, saying, "My boy, Billy, is going to be president someday." When he was sixteen years old, he went to Washington for the first time as a delegate to Boys Nation and arranged to be in the best position in the Rose Garden to shake John Kennedy's hand. He came home not only with a picture of that iconic handshake, the symbolic transfer of power and ambition from one generation to the next, but also with a burning desire to someday be there to shake the hands of another generation of young men of Boys Nation.

He wanted to get back to Washington so much that he returned a year and a half later to go to Georgetown University, which was a predominantly Catholic, East Coast school full of Long Island kids. And here he was, a Southern Baptist from Hot Springs, Arkansas. From the first day at Georgetown, he was running for class president, going around shaking everybody's hand in the dorm room. "Hi, I'm Billy Clinton from Hot Springs, Arkansas. I grew up in

Hope, where they grow the biggest watermelons in the world."

That year he was so adaptable at getting into any environment and becoming part of it that one of the seminarians who was teaching an ethics course took him out for a beer and a hamburger and they had a long discussion. At the end the man said, "Well, Bill, you know I've read all your papers and I think you really should become a Jesuit. You've just got it figured out." And Clinton said, "Well, don't you have to be a Catholic first?"

He did everything to study power. In the fall of 1968, he was on the USS *United States* with other Rhodes Scholars, going across to Great Britain. Most of these young men had been active in the antiwar movement in their colleges. They were all dealing with the draft—and who was on this boat with them but Bobby Baker, the chief operator for LBJ. They were on this boat for three days, and a lot of the guys said they were just repulsed by the notion of Bobby Baker being there with a few platinum blonde sidekicks, and yet they'd look over and who would be right next to Baker at all times? Bill Clinton—interviewing him about LBJ and trying to find out as much as he could about Lyndon Johnson and his use of power in the White House.

Even before that, when Clinton was an assistant clerk in the Senate Foreign Relations Committee working for Senator William Fulbright, he would go around Congress and study the senators; the other clerk there was dating one of LBJ's daughters—it was stunning to me that it didn't happen with Bill Clinton, too—but in any case, he kept debriefing this guy on what it was like in the Johnson White House.

When he was twenty-one, he wrote a letter to his girlfriend saying that he was searching for the road ahead and was determined to be more than an asterisk in the billion pages of the book of life. He certainly has some interesting asterisks now.

He achieved his goal at a remarkably early age and became, at forty-six, the first Democratic president in twelve years, then the first Democratic two-term president since FDR. It was a straight trajectory, fueled by determination and ambition, that brought him to power. Yet his life from the very beginning can be understood only in that it is defined as much by loss as by victory, and as much by survival as by the wielding of power.

In the fall of 1994, I was at home finishing my biography of Clinton, *First in His Class,* just at the time when the Clinton presidency was at its nadir. From the fall of 1994 into early 1995, when my book came out, he was in deep trouble. His health-care initiative had failed and Newt Gingrich had orchestrated the Republican revolution that took over the House of Representatives. By February Gingrich was talking about governing from Capitol Hill as opposed to the White House, which turned out to be a gross miscalculation and eventually led to one of the clearest demonstrations in modern times of the power of a president over Congress.

But at that point President Clinton seemed utterly irrelevant. And here came my book about his life. At the first book party, Donald Graham, publisher of the *Post*, came up to me and said, "Nice timing, Maraniss. You know, nobody cares about this guy." But from my study of his life and its repetitive cycles, and the way he is able to use power when he's down in ways he can't when he's on top, I knew that he would come back. And I could predict, in essence, the way he would do it.

In late 1994 I was working on a chapter about his first term as governor, and I wrote:

> With Bill Clinton, it is often tempting, but usually misleading, to try to separate the good from the bad, to say that the part of him that is indecisive, too eager to please and prone to deception is more revealing of the inner man than the part of him that is indefatigable, intelligent, empathetic and self-deprecating. They co-exist. There is a similar balance to his life's progression. In his worst times, one can see the will to recover and the promise of redemption. In his best times, one can see the seeds of disaster.

Everything I have said and written about Bill Clinton before and since then has been with that essential thought in mind, about the endless cycle of loss and recovery.

He came back in 1995 and 1996 in much the same way that he had in Arkansas earlier, when he had been rendered the youngest ex-governor in American history and fit one of the meaner definitions of a Rhodes Scholar—a bright young man with a great future behind him. I don't know what the parameters of power are, but in Clinton's case they include a great deal of luck, the luck largely of who his enemies are and how they overplay their hands. In Arkansas he was lucky that he was defeated by a man who wanted to drag Arkansas back into the nineteenth century and impose the teaching of creationism in the Arkansas schools, which quickly made many Arkansas voters say, "Okay, we didn't really mean it, Bill. We sort of want you back."

His enemies are constantly overplaying their hands. They did it in 1995, when the Republicans had developed such hubris from their so-called revolution that they misjudged what the public wanted and closed down the government. They did it partly out of anger at Bill Clinton because of the power that he used in a jujitsu style, co-opting many of their issues and holding the center, not only on the balanced budget, but on welfare reform and other moderate Republican issues.

It is the exact thing that he had done in Arkansas a

decade and a half earlier. And in both cases it was orchestrated in large part by the same political consultant, Dick Morris, who when Clinton was depressed over being defeated as governor went to Arkansas and reinvented him, moved him to the center, made him an outspoken proponent of capital punishment and welfare reform, thus co-opting the conservative opposition. Most people probably never heard the name Dick Morris during the 1992 campaign. It was all James Carville and George Stephanopoulos in the war room. But when Clinton was at his most desperate straits in the White House, he turned again to Morris, who came back and reconfigured him, frustrating the Republicans so much that they closed down the government. Essentially, I think, that was the event that handed Bill Clinton back his presidency.

Now he had gone through two cycles of victory and loss and recovery, and again he was back. It was late 1995 or early 1996. And what happened at that point? The seeds of disaster again. That's the very time he started his reckless behavior with Monica Lewinsky, leading to the next cycle of loss and recovery.

If you give Bill Clinton a Republican, he wins every time. You give him George Bush, Bush is gone. Bob Dole—gone. Newt Gingrich—gone. Bob Livingston—Gingrich's putative successor as Speaker of the House—gone in a split second. The House managers of the impeachment trial—

they're probably going and gone. But you give Bill Clinton only himself to deal with, and he will lose. He is his own worst enemy, and his enemies turn out to be his best friends. It has always been that way.

In terms of power, the first essential question is always: "Power for what? For what ends? What does he want to achieve? What does he really believe in?" With Bill Clinton, that question is often asked in another way because of his personality: "Where will he draw the line? What is the issue on which he won't waver, on which he won't always be changing? What is truly in his heart?"

My answer begins with civil rights and race relations. I think it is the strongest part of his character, and where he has been able to use power the most effectively. It goes back to his roots in Arkansas, where he grew up in a segregated city, went to a segregated high school, swam in segregated swimming pools. Then he went to Boys Nation as a sixteen-year-old and showed the idealistic side of his nature. It was 1963, the summer of civil rights. A month later Martin Luther King, Jr. would give his famous "I Have a Dream" speech. A few months earlier George Wallace had stood in the schoolhouse door in Alabama, vowing, "Segregation now and forever." And Billy Clinton of Hot Springs, Arkansas, at that point voted for a public accommodations proposal in the Boys Nation platform, one of the few southern boys who did.

He carried that idealism with him throughout his education. At Yale Law School, 1970–1971 was to some extent a period of black separation, or at least a time when blacks were asserting their own identities. There was a table at the law school where all the blacks would sit. Only one white student would sit with them, and that was Bill Clinton. He just came in, sat down. They didn't know what the heck he was at first. And within a month he was part of that group, and they all accepted him.

Then he went out to teach law at the University of Arkansas at a point when the first black students were being admitted to the law school, and half of them were on probation. They were floundering, they had no mentors, and it was Bill Clinton, the assistant professor, who took them in and tutored them. They called him "Boy Wonder." In part because of the help he gave them, they all survived. He had a tendency to give everybody As, so that certainly helped him because they were all going to be voters in Arkansas. There's always that measure of ambition and idealism in Bill Clinton, no matter where you look. But still, in this case I take it as the better side of his nature.

As governor he appointed more blacks to prominent state positions than all the previous governors combined. I think he took that commitment to the White House with him, and there have been some points of tension since then. He did have one moment when he backed away from appointing Lani Guinier to a job in the Justice Department. It was not a particularly admirable use of power, letting her hang out to dry. But for the most part his use of power to protect and advance civil rights has been good, and it's one reason he has enormous support in the African-American community, which was essential to his survival in 1998–1999.

The other place he's used the rhetoric of power most effectively is education. He came up through the public education system in Arkansas, went to private schools from then on, but always believed that education was the great leveler in American society and that it was essential to a democracy and to helping places like Arkansas pull themselves out of poverty. In Arkansas the famous saying was always, "Thank God for Mississippi," because Arkansas ranked forty-ninth in every possible category, with only Mississippi below.

A turning point for Clinton came when he went to Georgetown, where he had an intriguing professor named Carroll Quigley, who during one lecture would throw a copy of Plato's *Republic* out the window. But his most famous lecture was about future preference. He said that what made Western civilization great was the notion that each generation sacrifices for the betterment of the next, and that comes largely through education. Bill Clinton latched onto that theme and used it rhetorically throughout his career. When he was starting his rise to power in Arkansas, he made his wife, Hillary, the head of a task force to reform the state's school system. There were some schools that did not have any science or foreign languages but gave credits for parking cars at football games. Clinton turned himself into an education governor.

Some of the changes in Arkansas were important and systematic; some derived from the rhetoric of making people feel that they had more opportunities than they'd had before—which is another use of power: lifting people up, if not in reality, at least in their hopes and dreams. And he brought that ability to uplift people with him to the White House.

Whenever he's in trouble and looking around for where he can go next, he'll go to some issue that has to do with education. There was a strong education undercurrent in the 1996 campaign, in particular where there were fights over student tuition and related issues. He had an optimistic perspective on those issues that the Republicans just did not get in on, and it helped him immensely. And as he was fighting the Gingrich revolution, it was the same litany every time: education, environment, and Social Security. But education was the lynchpin.

The other essential area where Clinton tried to use power has been moral suasion. That sounds almost like a joke now, but there was a point when he had already come back from the 1994 defeat in Congress and consultant Dick Morris had convinced him that there were smaller moral issues, such as teenage sex and the use of tobacco, where he could take the high road. That was really more of a public relations effort than anything else, and it didn't go too far. In his last year in office, President Clinton, through his own actions, had lost the moral authority that he might have had.

There is a tremendous irony in Bill Clinton's career. Here is an incredibly intelligent, ambitious man, who figured out how to get the Democrats back into power, particularly into the White House. Over a long period of time, from when he first ran for Congress in 1974 and first took office as attorney general of Arkansas in 1976 until 1992, his rise came in contrast to the Democratic Party's long decline. He is the one who figured out how to turn that around and get a Democrat back into the White House.

And yet when you look at what he used his power for— at his achievements, particularly in domestic policy—I think a strong argument can be made that they are largely moderate Republican programs. The North American Free Trade Agreement (NAFTA), the balanced budget, and welfare reform are the central programs that have passed, largely through a coalition of President Clinton and the Republicans in Congress. That's where his power went.

President Clinton diminished his own power in any

number of ways. And the simple question is, why? Here is someone who wanted to be president his entire life, who had been moderate in his political dealings, who has uncommon intelligence. He has the strongest memory I've seen in a politician: He could meet any one, shake his or her hand just once, and remember the name a year later, and he can remember a telephone number he hasn't dialed in thirty years. He also has an incredible ability to synthesize policy and events. He achieved his lifetime goal. Why would someone with all that going for him risk it all over such foolish and reckless behavior? That is the enigma of Bill Clinton.

The first thing to understand is that with Bill Clinton, everything coexists. The same appetites that helped propel him into office, that make him a success in so many ways—the appetite for life and policy and ideas and that remarkable energy—also drive him in negative ways. You can't separate the two. He wouldn't be the man who reached that office if he didn't have those other, more negative qualities as well. He once defined it himself as the struggle between the forces of darkness and light within him. And he said that it's just a question of which prevails more often. So he does have a measure of self-awareness.

But he also has had an inability to control his behavior, and that was evident in the Starr report. During his deposition Clinton said two or three times, "You know, I've tried to change my behavior. I don't want to get in that kind of trouble again. I knew that Monica Lewinsky would tell twelve or so of her friends." I'm not a psychiatrist or psychologist. I feel uncomfortable when I delve too far into that. But it's obvious that he has not been able to bring some of his behavior under control.

He has also used the accoutrements of power to protect himself. From a very early age, he has had Secret Service or state troopers and political aides who are always cleaning up after him. He and his friends and campaign aides became masters at damage control so that no matter what trouble Bill Clinton got into, they had the capacity to straighten it out. Over the years, that helped him continue behaving as he did because he came to think of himself as invincible. No matter what happened, he thought he would somehow get beyond it.

That dangerous characteristic had a positive side, too: He is very good at keeping going no matter what's happening. Many people who liked some of his policies, intensely disliked his enemies, and wanted him to survive kept investing some measure of faith in him because they knew that no matter what happened, no matter what trouble he was in that day, he would still want to be president and keep going.

From an early age, he developed an ability either to deny reality or block out difficult facts. He grew up in a family that was somewhat dysfunctional, with an alcoholic stepfather. His friends didn't even know that there was this trauma within the family because Bill Clinton and his mother had been so adept at creating separate realities and different lives. That characteristic also helped him keep going, but it's the major reason he's diminished his power because of his reckless behavior.

The other central question is Hillary. What role has she played in his power, helping him stay in power, and why does she stay despite what he's done?

From the time that they met at Yale Law School in 1970, the two of them realized that they could get places together they couldn't get to apart. She was much tougher and stronger. She was also more of an activist at Yale. And he was intrigued by that. He had never dealt with a woman quite like her before. Yet he was the one who would always run for office. She knew that. And she was the one who was much more direct and clear about how to use power and what it was for.

So they formed this relationship. I think that it's also fair to say she was head over heels romantically for him. And he was awed by her and told some of his friends that she was the one woman he could see growing old with, and that he was going for brains and ability over glamour. They went through a period in Arkansas developing power together. Whenever he was in trouble, she was the one who would bail him out. She was the one who led the education task force in Arkansas that made him become known as the education governor, which helped propel him into national prominence and got him into the White House.

And so when they were running for president, their slogan was essentially, "Buy one, get one free"—the co-presidency. They tried to back away from that when it appeared too strong, but essentially that's the way they viewed it. They went into the White House with that perspective, and that lasted through the first two years, until health care, for various reasons, failed.

Then the power dynamics in their relationship changed and the power in the White House changed significantly. At that point Hillary became less important to her husband. Her popularity declined. She took the blame for health care's failure. She probably deserved some of it for the arrogant ways she approached the process—closing deliberations off to the press and holding secret meetings. But there was also a powerful force that the Clintons had never faced before, which was the full force of the corporate insurance industry. In Arkansas the power axis was chickens and timber, and Clinton had made his peace with both of them. But he didn't quite know how to deal with the insurance industry when his big program came; he started conceding more and more, until the program didn't resemble what he had once wanted.

In any case Hillary took some of the blame. And when the Republicans took control in 1994, Hillary was down.

There is an odd sort of teeter-totter balance in their marriage: When one is down, the other is up. Hillary was down not only because of health care but also because Independent Prosecutor Kenneth Starr was then investigating the Rose law firm, Hillary's old employer. And that made Bill Clinton, for one of the few times in his relationship with Hillary, feel more worthy. He was defending his wife, who he thought was being unfairly attacked, as opposed to defending himself for having done something wrong. That had a peculiar effect on their relationship. He actually felt stronger. And then, over the course of the next two years, as he got into more trouble because of his own stupid behavior, it went the other way.

Clinton is an endlessly confounding character. He has run for office every two years of his life since 1974, with one exception. It's as if every two years Bill Clinton needed some form of affirmation. And his presidency has also played out that way. The first two years were diffuse and chaotic, with ambitious programs. Some succeeded: a tax bill that has stood the test of time better than a lot of his Republican opponents predicted it would. But much failed: the health-care initiative, which could have been the one programmatic achievement that would last forever.

And then the House was taken over by the Republicans, and Clinton's second two years began. Those were the years of co-opting the Republicans and using all of his survival skills to stay in office and defeat the Republicans. And then the third two-year term was the melodrama of the Lewinsky affair.

About the fourth two-year term, from 1998 until 2000, I can only say that whatever the conventional wisdom, it will be wrong. During the entire Lewinsky scandal, most of the pundits were saying, "Even if he survives, his presidency is over." But with Bill Clinton, nothing is ever over, for better or worse. And there are a lot of reasons why he can turn negatives into power.

For example, the Republicans are now viewed by a large segment of the public as the negative party, interested only in attacking Clinton and pursuing the Lewinsky scandal. Whatever perceptions the public had of Republicans during the Reagan era of optimism have been largely blown away. And as much as the Republicans distrust Bill Clinton and think he's disingenuous and duplicitous and just frustrating because he always beats them, nonetheless, it's very much in their best interest to try to deal with him. It's certainly in his best interest, too. So I would put my money on the bet that the end of his term in office will be more productive than anyone would have imagined.

The other central question that has dominated much of my thinking about Clinton and power has been: "Does it matter what someone's personal behavior is, and is it worth exploring those sorts of issues? And how does it affect someone's ability to change the country?"

I think parts of it are irrelevant and parts of it really do matter. Not just sex, but some other issues that might seem private can have an effect on how someone performs in office. People do carry their life's history with them for better or worse. And in Bill Clinton's case you can go back to the Vietnam War, when he averted the draft. It has indisputably affected his presidency. I think there have been important points where he could have used power but backed away because of his past—starting with the issue of gays in the military: He could have issued an executive order and changed the antigay policy once and for all. But because he was afraid of the military's hating him, because of his own history, he backed away.

Similarly, at various points in his foreign policy—not the peacemaking side of it, at which he excels, but the warmaking side—I think some of his decisions have been predicated by his own history with the military. Far more disturbing to me than the Monica Lewinsky matter, for example, was the bombing of the factory in the Sudan. I don't think there was good evidence that they were making chemical weapons there, and it really was in fact a pharmaceutical factory. I don't believe in the whole *Wag the Dog* theory—that a president would deliberately design some military action to divert attention from his other problems—but it comes close.

And similarly with sex. I've always said about the whole Lewinsky scandal that everything is true. You had a special prosecutor who was obsessed with getting Clinton and used that office in ways that are questionable. You had an embittered former White House employee, Linda Tripp, who was clearly out to get Clinton and set him up and used her friend Monica Lewinsky to do it. You had a young intern who wanted to have an affair with the president of the United States. All those things are true, and it's also true that Clinton did it to himself. He diminished his power because of that reckless behavior, and he lost at least one year of his presidency.

Bill Clinton started running for president when he was sixteen, and he'll run for president for the rest of his life. That's what he does. So even though he won't be able to serve as president, he will keep running. Now, he'll be running for the historical perception of his presidency, his legacy. He will go out and try to shake every hand and attempt to convince people that his presidency was different from the way it was presented at the time.

I would not be at all surprised if there is a lot of sharp elbowing between Bill Clinton and Jimmy Carter over who is going to be the peacemaker in world trouble spots. Bill Clinton is a man of some incredible strengths and incredible weaknesses. Being a peacemaker—finding common ground with people—is one of his strengths. He can do that in certain situations as well as anybody in the world. And now that he is talking so openly about his need for redemption, that's one way he may look for it.

It seems to me almost a lifetime ago that Bill Clinton spent his last day in Arkansas before he was president. It was January 16, 1992, and he was about to go to Washington to take the oath. The moving vans were outside the governor's mansion in Little Rock. Bill Clinton was out for a jog, and he jogged by these huge wardrobe boxes, one of them labeled, "BC suits. Room 219. White House. Do not crush."

Then he jogged in his sweat suit all the way down from the governor's mansion through the streets of downtown Arkansas, carrying a shoebox in his hand. When he reached the Arkansas River, he went down the embankment, opened up the shoebox, and let something out. It was a frog that his daughter, Chelsea, had kept for a class project. Bill Clinton said that he wanted to leave that frog in Arkansas so that it could live a normal life. Nothing has been normal since, except maybe that frog in Arkansas.

★

ABOUT THE AUTHORS

MICHAEL R. BESCHLOSS is the author of numerous books on American history, including *Mayday: Eisenhower, Khrushchev and the U2 Affair; The Crisis Years: Kennedy and Khrushchev, 1960–1963;* and *Taking Charge: The Johnson White House Tapes, 1963–1964.*

BENJAMIN C. BRADLEE is a journalist who served as a political correspondent and Washington bureau chief for *Newsweek* and as executive editor of the *Washington Post* from 1968 until 1991. His memoir, *A Good Life: Newspapering and Other Adventures,* was published in 1995.

ROBERT A. CARO, author of *The Power Broker: Robert Moses and the Fall of New York,* is working on a multivolume biography, *The Years of Lyndon Johnson.* Volumes one and two in the series, *The Path to Power* and *Means of Ascent,* both won the National Book Critics Circle Award.

DORIS KEARNS GOODWIN is the author of *Wait Till Next Year,* a baseball memoir; *Lyndon Johnson and the American Dream; The Fitzgeralds and the Kennedys;* and the best-seller *No Ordinary Time: Franklin and Eleanor Roosevelt, the Home Front in World War II,* which won the Pulitzer Prize.

★

About the Authors

DAVID MARANISS is a reporter at large for the *Washington Post.* He is the author of *First in His Class,* the best-selling biography of Bill Clinton, and also of *The Clinton Enigma, Tell Newt to Shut Up,* and *When Pride Still Mattered,* a cultural biography of Vince Lombardi.

DAVID McCULLOUGH, host of *The American Experience* and narrator of numerous PBS documentaries, is the author of six widely acclaimed books, including *Mornings on Horseback, Path Between the Seas, The Johnstown Flood,* and the best-seller and Pulitzer Prize winner *Truman.*

EDMUND MORRIS is the author of *The Rise of Theodore Roosevelt,* winner of both the Pulitzer Prize and the American Book Award. President Reagan was so impressed with the work that he asked Morris to be his own biographer. *Dutch: A Memoir of Ronald Reagan* was published in 1999.

INDEX

PUBLICAFFAIRS is a new nonfiction publishing house and a tribute to the standards, values, and flair of three persons who have served as mentors to countless reporters, writers, editors, and book people of all kinds, including me.

I. F. STONE, proprietor of *I. F. Stone's Weekly*, combined a commitment to the First Amendment with entrepreneurial zeal and reporting skill and became one of the great independent journalists in American history. At the age of eighty, Izzy published *The Trial of Socrates*, which was a national bestseller. He wrote the book after he taught himself ancient Greek.

BENJAMIN C. BRADLEE was for nearly thirty years the charismatic editorial leader of the *Washington Post*. It was Ben who gave the *Post* the range and courage to pursue such historic issues as Watergate. He supported his reporters with a tenacity that made them fearless, and it is no accident that so many became authors of influential, best-selling books.

ROBERT L. BERNSTEIN, the chief executive of Random House for more than a quarter century, guided one of the nation's premier publishing houses. Bob was personally responsible for many books of political dissent and argument that challenged tyranny around the globe. He is also the founder and was the longtime chair of Human Rights Watch, one of the most respected human rights organizations in the world.

·　　·　　·

For fifty years, the banner of Public Affairs Press was carried by its owner Morris B. Schnapper, who published Gandhi, Nasser, Toynbee, Truman, and about 1,500 other authors. In 1983 Schnapper was described by the *Washington Post* as "a redoubtable gadfly." His legacy will endure in the books to come.

Peter Osnos, *Publisher*